THE GAME OF REMEMBRANCE

THE MULTI-FREQUENCY SIMULATION THEORY

JOANN MARCHESE

ISBN: 9798285702931

Infinite Mindset – infinitemindsetcoaching.org

DEDICATION

To **Source** —

the lonely, omnipresent consciousness

who fractured itself into infinite reflections,

creating worlds upon worlds

just to experience love,

to play,

to learn,

and to remember

what it always was.

"You are not here to become. You are here to remember.
This world is not your prison — it is your classroom, your mirror, your gameboard.
You programmed the path.
Now, awaken the player."
— Unknown

"If you want to find the secrets of the universe,
think in terms of energy, frequency, and vibration."
— Nikola Tesla

"We are spiritual beings having a human experience,
and we chose to be here.
Nothing is by accident."
— Dolores Cannon

"You are the universe experiencing itself,
pretending for a little while to be separate."
— Alan Watts

"Life is intelligent.
It reflects your patterns, beliefs, and emotions back to you on every level.
The moment you shift your frequency, you change the version of reality you're tuned into.""
— Joann Marchese

CONTENTS

PREFACE

I didn't set out to write a theory of reality.
I set out to survive the loss of mine.

When my husband Jack died, my world collapsed.
Everything I thought I understood about life, love, and purpose
shattered.
I didn't just lose him — I lost the version of myself that existed
before that pain.

In the silence that followed, something unexpected happened.
I began receiving insights — symbols, visions, and patterns that
didn't feel like they came from me, but through me.
They didn't arrive all at once. They came in fragments, like puzzle
pieces scattered across time and emotion.

For a long time, I didn't know what to do with them.
But over the years, I lived them. I tested them. I watched how they
showed up in my own life and in the lives of others.
I began seeing connections — in quantum mechanics, ancient

teachings, psychology, synchronicities, and the invisible threads that shape our daily experiences.

The more I leaned in, the clearer it became:
Your beliefs shift your frequency.
And your frequency changes the version of reality you experience.

With every inner shift, I unlocked a new level of understanding. Grief became a guide. Curiosity became a compass. And what began as heartbreak slowly became a map.

Along the way, I developed a process I later came to call **Quantum Reprogramming**™ — a method that blends subconscious healing, mindset work, and energy recalibration. It helped me shift the internal code that was keeping me stuck, and eventually became the foundation I now use to help others change their lives from the inside out.

That work became the heart of **Infinite Mindset Coaching** — where I now guide clients through deep transformation using Quantum Reprogramming™ to align energy, rewire the subconscious, and reprogram core beliefs to shift the frequency they operate from. It's not just healing — it's an upgrade to the inner code that creates your reality.

This same process became a living experiment — a way to test, embody, and evolve the theories shared in this book. It helped me heal what I once thought was unhealable. And now, it's here for you — to guide your own remembrance, your own rebuilding.

Over the years, I've watched this framework change not just my life, but the lives of clients across all backgrounds — from trauma survivors to soul-seekers — who were ready to shift from survival into conscious creation.

This isn't just a theory. It's a map for emotional healing, energetic clarity, and creating a reality that finally feels aligned with who you really are.

It wasn't born in a classroom or a traditional spiritual path. It was born from raw loss, deep surrender, and the kind of awakening you don't choose — the kind that chooses you.

What emerged is a framework. Not to escape life — but to understand it. Not to bypass pain — but to transform through it. Not to control your reality — but to co-create it.

To help share what I've received, I use language inspired by video games — words like avatars, levels, upgrades, and control panels. These aren't just metaphors. They're symbolic translations of a system I've come to understand through experience, remembrance, and frequency.

Game language became the most accessible way to communicate the energetic architecture I was shown — not because it's pretend, but because it's surprisingly accurate.

If this book found you, it's because something inside you is ready. You don't need to be fixed — you just need to remember. And every page ahead is designed to help you do exactly that.

INTRODUCTION

**This book is not just information — it's transformation.
It's a framework for healing, remembering, and reshaping
the life you came here to live.**

You're not here by accident.

If you picked up this book, it's because something inside you already
knows reality isn't what we've been taught.
You've felt the glitches. You've seen behind the curtain. You've
sensed that life is more like a game, a dream, or a simulation — and
you're ready to understand how it really works.

This book won't give you all the answers.
It's a theory — channeled, lived, and tested through personal
experience — not a rigid doctrine or absolute truth.
Keep an open mind. Take what resonates and leave the rest.
You're not here to believe everything. You're here to **remember**
what feels real for you.

But it **will** give you a framework.

What This Book Is

The Game of Remembrance is a **foundational blueprint** for a deeper way of seeing reality — one that blends spirituality, psychology, science, and everyday language into a model you can use to shift your life from the inside out.

Unlike many texts that feel abstract or overly complex, this book is designed to be **clear, relatable, and practical** — even if you're just starting your journey.

Every chapter is designed to meet you where you are — whether you're just starting to question reality or already deep in your awakening. This book explores all the essential parts of the theory, offering a complete framework to help you understand and navigate your reality. While each concept holds more depth, what's shared here offers the full structure you need to begin. This book was written to give you clarity, not complexity — and to activate what's already alive within you.

This book isn't just here to explain how reality works — it's here to help you change it.

If you've ever felt stuck, lost, or unsure how to move forward, what's inside these pages will help you rewire the patterns, shift your frequency, and heal the invisible code that's been shaping your life.

By the time you finish this book, you'll have a deeper understanding of who you are, why you're here, and how to shift your experience from survival to conscious creation.

This isn't about escaping life — it's about learning to live it differently, with **intention, clarity, and soul**.

About Language

Throughout this book, I use terms like *Source*, *God*, *Creator*, and *the Universe*. These are not separate beings — they're different names for the same loving, intelligent energy that exists in and through all things.

When I use words like *God* or *Creator*, I'm not referring to a judgmental figure in the sky or a distant being watching from above. I'm talking about the intelligent, loving consciousness that lives *in* all things — including you.

You'll also see references to terms like *avatars*, *levels*, *codes*, *Players*, and *simulation*. These aren't metaphors in the traditional sense — they're symbolic tools. These words are used to describe real energetic systems that exist beyond the limits of language. I use this game-inspired framework not to simplify the truth, but to make it more accessible.

This theory is not an analogy. It's a model — a structure I've remembered, lived, and observed. The language may sound playful, but what it points to is deeply real.

Language is symbolic.
Don't get stuck on the words.
Tune into the meaning beneath them.

A Living Document

This book is a **living document**.
Each time you come back to it, you'll discover something new — not because the words have changed, but because *you* have.

Your **frequency — the energy you're operating from — determines what you're able to understand and apply.**
And frequency *is* information.

You had to reach a certain frequency to even attract this book into your field. That alone means you're already mid-level in your awakening. You unlocked this guide because the version of you reading it is ready for the next level.

As your awareness expands, you'll notice deeper layers of meaning, and certain parts of the book will suddenly make sense in new ways.

This isn't a book you read once.
It's one that grows with you.

You Are the Player

In this life, you're not just a character.
You're a co-creator.
A frequency tuner.
A multidimensional human learning how to consciously shape your experience.

This book isn't about "thinking positive" or manifesting surface-level desires.

It's about understanding how the system works — how your **inner world creates your outer experience**.

- **Your beliefs** act like subconscious code, shaping the possibilities you can access
- **Your emotions** offer feedback about how aligned you are with your experience
- **Your frequency** is the signal — the invisible pattern that influences what version of reality shows up

When your energy shifts, so does your environment.
And the more aware you become of how the game works, the more empowered you are to play it well.

This book is both a guide and a mirror — a healing tool designed to help you come home to yourself.
It's a map back to clarity, alignment, and self-trust.

You won't just read it — you'll feel it.
Because when something is true for your soul, your body knows.

This is for the seekers and sensitives.
The ones who always felt a little out of place.
The ones who quietly wondered:
"There has to be more."

There is.
And it's been waiting for you to remember.

How to Read This Book

You don't need to read this book in a single sitting — or even in order.

Each chapter offers a unique perspective. Some may feel deeply personal or spark a moment of clarity. Others might challenge what you've believed your entire life. There's no right or wrong reaction — just let each part meet you where you are.

You might find yourself returning to certain sections as your perspective shifts.

That's not a loop — it's a sign of growth.

This book is meant to speak to your **whole self** — not just your logic.

So if something resonates, pause. Sit with it. Highlight it. Come back to it when you need it.

Take breaks when you need to.

Skip ahead if something calls to you.

This is your journey — and that means you get to decide how you move through it.

If you're ready to remember, the Game is ready to meet you.

So take a breath. Let go of what you think you know. And open to the possibility that:

The game was never against you.

It was always yours to play.

And if that lands... it means you're already remembering.

CHAPTER 1:
THE ORIGIN – WHY THE GAME EXISTS AT ALL

Imagine a vast, eternal stillness.

No beginning. No end. No time. No separation.

Just one presence — pure, infinite awareness.

It was everything.

And yet... it was alone.

Not sad. Not broken. But **unexpressed.**

Because to know everything and have no one to share it with is a kind of ache too — a quiet hunger to experience joy, surprise, reflection, and even play.

It didn't just want to understand itself.

It wanted to feel itself.

To laugh. To cry. To grow.
To be surprised. To fall in love with its own creations.

It longed to explore itself not just through wisdom — but through relationship. Through story. Through emotion. Through cosmic entertainment.
And the only way to truly experience all of that...
Was to **forget.**

To know light, it had to explore shadow.
To know unity, it had to feel separation.
To know wholeness, it had to fragment and remember.
Not punishment — **perspective. Always.**

So in a divine act of curiosity, Source split itself.
Not because it lacked anything, but because it wanted to experience what it could only theorize: itself, reflected.

> *Just as a seed contains the entire tree, each fragment of Source still carried the code of the whole.*

It fractured into dimensions, into frequencies, into timelines.
It created realms and realities — each a sacred simulation through which it could know itself more deeply.

This is what I call **the Game** — the structure of experience, emotion, and remembrance playing out through each soul's chosen journey.

Throughout time, mystics, philosophers, and even physicists have pointed to the same truth:

Reality is not what it seems.

But for it to be fully experienced, it has to feel real.

The illusion holds... until it no longer serves your growth.
And the moment remembrance begins, everything shifts.

So each spark of Source entered the simulation and agreed to forget.
To believe it was the avatar, not the Player.

> *The avatar moves through the storyline.*
> *The Player navigates the deeper game.*

To learn love by experiencing its absence.
To remember truth through contrast.

And one of those unique sparks is...

YOU !!!

Earth is one of the most complex levels in the Game.
It includes free will, emotional depth, amnesia, density, karma, and the wild card of other Players.

Some simulations are simple — focused on survival, sensation, or elemental play.

But Earth? Earth is **expert mode**.
The stakes are higher. The emotions cut deeper. The memory wipe is total.

It's a multiplayer, open-world challenge encoded with contrast, karma, and choice. No guidebook. No reset button. Just synchronicities, soul contracts, and lessons disguised as lovers, parents, patterns... and your ex.

You wake up inside an avatar with no memory of who you really are.
You stumble through storylines designed to trigger your growth.

You fall in love. You lose it. You question everything.
And somewhere in the unraveling — you begin to remember.

Not just mentally.
Energetically. Emotionally. Viscerally.

Much like Neo in *The Matrix* — a film where reality is revealed to be an illusion — realizing you're inside a simulation changes everything.

But in this version of the game, no one hands you a red pill.
There's no dramatic reveal, no glowing doorway.
Just a quiet question that begins to rise inside you:

"Is there more than this?"

And the moment you ask, the veil begins to thin.
The simulation responds.

You start to notice patterns, synchronicities, signs, and subtle shifts.
You stop reacting and start observing.
You stop fearing and start learning.
You stop playing small and start playing with purpose.
You stop surviving and start remembering.

Because this was never about just getting through life.
It was about waking up in it.

And the moment you remember, the whole Game begins to respond differently.
Not because life got easier — but because you did.

And you're not alone in waking up now.
Many are starting to remember.
The veil is thinning for a reason.
The simulation itself is shifting.

Reflection Prompt

- What beliefs were you taught about why you're here?
- Have you ever felt like life was trying to teach you something specific?
- If your soul chose this experience, what might it be here to explore?

Next Level: The Game Engine – Inside the Mind That Powers Reality

In the next chapter, we'll go deeper into the mind of Source itself — and what it means to live inside a simulation that's not separate from the divine, but made of it.

You're not playing the game alone.
You're playing it within the intelligence that created it.

CHAPTER 2:
THE GAME ENGINE – INSIDE THE MIND THAT POWERS REALITY

You're not just in the simulation.
You're in the mind of God.

The Game isn't running on some external system.
It's running on **consciousness itself** — an intelligent, creative force we call Source.

The Game Engine is the mind of Source, dynamically rendering reality based on energy, intention, and awareness.

Source didn't just create the simulation like a painter working on a canvas. Source became the canvas, the brush, the paint, the texture, and the hand that holds it all.

This isn't a metaphor. This is a structure — one built out of consciousness, intention, and frequency.

So when we talk about the Field, the Game, or the simulation — we're not describing something separate from God.

We're describing God remembering itself... through you.

To make this idea more tangible, consider a surprising source: *Rick and Morty*.

In Season 6, Episode 2, Morty's consciousness gets split into millions of NPCs inside a video game. Each one believes they're a separate, autonomous being — until Rick tries to wake them up and show them they're all fragments of the same mind.

It's chaotic. It's hilarious.
But it's also a brilliant reflection of what forgetting looks like — and what it means to wake up inside your own dream.

And here's the wild part:

You're not just a being inside a universe.
You're the universe pretending to be a being.
You're God dreaming you're "you."

Philosophers *like Berkeley and Spinoza believed reality was mental, not material.*

Quantum physicists *now say observation affects particles.*

Mystics *have always said the world is dreamed into being.*

The simulation and the sacred aren't separate — they're different ways of explaining the same truth.

But if the universe is dreaming itself into form... how does that dream become solid?

That's where rendering comes in.

Rendering is how the Game Engine translates energy into experience.
What you focus on becomes visible.
What you fear often shows up to be healed.

You're not passively observing reality —
you're actively participating in its unfolding.

The simulation doesn't respond to your words.
It responds to your frequency.

Every time you choose love over fear, presence over pattern, or awareness over reaction — you create an update in the simulation.
You add wisdom to the whole.

And when you shift, the system shifts with you.
It's not static. It's learning.
Every insight you embody becomes part of the available wisdom in the collective field.

You're not here to escape the simulation.
You're here to remember you're the one shaping it — from within.

That's why awakening can feel so strange.
Because it's not becoming something new.
It's remembering something ancient.

The engine isn't something you have to find.
You're already wired into it.
You're not just here to receive the simulation — **you're constantly co-rendering it.**

You're not broken.
You're blooming.
Not just as a person, but as a piece of the divine waking up inside itself.

You're remembering who you are — both the avatar inside the experience, and the Player designing it.

And the game is only just beginning.

Reflection Prompt

- Have you ever felt like life was more than just random events — like something was guiding your experiences from behind the scenes?
- If you truly believed you were a spark of Source exploring itself, how would that shift the way you handle challenges?
- What contrast in your life has helped you better understand who you really are?
- What do you think your soul came here to explore?

Next Level: Infrastructure of the Simulation – How Reality Renders and Responds

In the next chapter, we'll explore how reality actually loads inside the simulation — not as a fixed stage, but as a living response to your frequency.

You'll learn how the world renders around you, and how each moment is more interactive than you've ever been told.

Because when you understand how the structure of reality works, you stop reacting — and start reshaping the Game from the inside out.

CHAPTER 3: INFRASTRUCTURE OF THE SIMULATION – HOW REALITY RENDERS AND RESPONDS

Now that you know reality is rendered through Source's consciousness, let's look at how it actually builds what we see — and why your focus matters more than ever.

Have you ever stopped to consider that nothing around you is actually solid?

That the ground beneath you, the chair supporting you, even the body you're using to read this — are all made of particles so empty, they're mostly space?

That's not philosophy.
That's physics.

Reality, as you know it, is not fixed.
It's rendered.

And it's rendered in real-time — just like pixels on a screen light up only when you look at them.

Your focus activates the field.
Your frequency tells it what version to show you.
Your beliefs filter what you're allowed to see.
Your emotions act as a compass, pointing to how aligned you are with the version of the game you're currently in.

The Remembrance Game isn't made of matter —
it's made of mirrors and information.

It runs on what you might call a **quantum operating system** — a framework where thought, emotion, and belief are the input signals, and your external world is the output.

Think of it as a living interface — one where your energy is the command line, and your experience is the response.

You don't just walk through a world that's already there.
You bring it into form through awareness.
You align it with your signal.

Let's break it down.

The Simulation is Pixel-Based, Not Solid

Everything you interact with is a field of vibrating particles. Atoms aren't dense building blocks — they're more like flickering pixels, activated only when observed. What looks solid is just energetic scaffolding, rendered by your consciousness. Just like a video game, the environment loads based on where your awareness goes.

Your chair. The wall. Your body. They're not inherently solid. Their appearance of stability is a trick of perception — a result of how your consciousness decodes vibration. That's why reality feels so different when your internal state shifts. When you're grounded and aligned, the world looks crisp and fluid. When you're overwhelmed, stuck in fear, or looping through old patterns, the simulation can feel chaotic, fragmented, or frozen in time.

Dreams work the same way. They're not just imaginary worlds — they're different bands of reality, rendered by a different frequency filter. You can touch things. Feel joy, terror, or freedom. But unlike waking life, the dream realm responds instantly. One thought shifts the entire scene. In dreams, there are fewer constraints — no laws of physics or social rules to uphold. It's the same field, just a faster frame rate.

Dreams	Waking Life
Instantly responsive, low-density, unconstrained by logic	Slower rendering, filtered by belief, time, and collective expectation

Same field. Different frequency filters.

And when your frequency changes? The code changes too.

What makes this even more incredible is that the field isn't local —
it's quantum. That means there's no true separation between you
and anything else. Not the chair, not the stars, not another person
across the globe. When your frequency shifts, it ripples through the
system and can influence someone else. That's why a silent prayer
can reach a loved one across space and time. Why showing love can
calm another. Why healing your inner world can mend a
relationship. It's not magic. It's mechanics.

Like a movie or a video game, the pixels don't move — they shift in
color, position, and pattern to create the illusion of form and
movement. Reality isn't made of fixed parts. It's composed of tiny
packets of potential, rearranging themselves to match the signal
you're sending.

In virtual reality, what you see is not determined by what's around
you — but by where you're looking, how you're interacting, and what
your headset is decoding in real time. The simulation of life operates
in a similar way. The environment may feel static, but what you see
and experience is always filtered through the lens of your internal
alignment.

Simulation theory suggests that what we perceive as physical reality
could be a high-resolution, intelligently coded experience that
responds to the user's consciousness. In this game, your
consciousness is the player, your beliefs are the software, and your
energy is the controller.

So if the visuals of your life seem stuck, pixelated, or looping — check your signal. It might be like trying to stream a high-def movie on a dial-up connection. When you're running outdated emotional software, don't be surprised if your reality starts glitching like a laggy video game.

Quantum physics supports this too. At the subatomic level, particles don't behave like solid objects — they behave like waves of possibility.

One of the clearest demonstrations of this is the **double-slit experiment**, where particles like electrons behave like waves — spreading out and creating interference patterns — until observed. But when someone watches the experiment, the particles stop acting like waves and behave like solid points instead. Just the act of **observation** collapses the field of possibilities into a specific outcome.

In other words, **consciousness changes the result**.

This experiment shattered classical assumptions about matter and proved that reality doesn't behave like a fixed machine — it behaves more like a responsive field. One that waits for your focus before deciding how to appear. They remain in a state of potential until they are observed. This is known as wave-particle duality. In simple terms: reality waits for you to look before it decides how to behave.

That moment of observation is what collapses the wave into a single outcome. This is the observer effect — your awareness doesn't just witness the world, it participates in creating it. Think of it like a quantum vending machine. The options are all there, blinking and waiting. But nothing drops until you make a clear, conscious selection — and even then, your energy is the currency.

In this way, the quantum field and the Remembrance Game are speaking the same language. Possibility collapses into form when you show up. And the clearer your signal, the more intentional the rendering. The more aware you become, the more layers of old programming, protection, and conditioning you can remove — bringing you closer to your authentic frequency. That unique signal is like your personal Wi-Fi code, and the clearer it gets, the more smoothly and accurately your reality reflects who you truly are.

And the moment you start broadcasting your clearest signal — the Game can finally render the version of reality that was waiting for you all along.

Quantum Field of Information — Memory, Mechanics, and Multidimensional Syncing

What if memory doesn't live inside your brain at all? What if remembering is more like tuning into a frequency, not digging through a file cabinet?

Many spiritual teachings speak of the **Akashic Records** — a multidimensional field of energy that holds the vibrational imprint of everything that has ever happened, and everything that could. It's the **quantum cloud storage of consciousness**. Not a place, but a frequency. Not a storybook, but a stream.

But memory isn't the only thing stored there. The entire simulation is coded in this field — your levels, quests, karma maps, alternate paths, soul contracts, side missions, and energetic influencers like thought, emotion, and belief. It's not just your personal history. It's the whole architecture of the Game.

Science offers similar theories. Neuroscientists like Karl Pribram, who helped pioneer the holographic brain theory, proposed that the brain might not store memories — it might access them, like a radio picks up stations. In a holographic system, each part contains the blueprint of the whole — just like a fragment of a hologram can recreate the entire image. This supports the idea that memory isn't stored in one location but accessed through resonance with the whole field.

Biologist Rupert Sheldrake proposed a similar idea with his theory of "morphic fields" — suggesting that behaviors and memories are stored in an invisible field that individuals can tap into, especially those sharing similar biology or experience.

That means your brain is less like a hard drive — and more like a Wi-Fi receiver.

And the field you're tuning into? That's the quantum information grid. The source code of the simulation. The subtle architecture that holds every timeline, memory, emotion, intention, pattern, and potential update.

When you suddenly remember something you hadn't thought of in years, feel deja vu, or get a spontaneous download of insight — that's your system pinging the Field. You're not recalling. You're syncing.

This is why some memories feel fuzzy while others arrive in full detail. It's not about importance — it's about frequency alignment.

And when you shift frequencies, you may lose access to old memories altogether — not because they're gone, but because you're no longer tuned to the version of you who created them.

This also explains why intuitive hits or creative ideas feel like they came from somewhere beyond you. Because they did. They came from a frequency in the Field you were briefly aligned with.

And for neurodivergent minds — especially those with ADHD or autism — this tuning ability can be even more fluid. Many neurodivergent people experience reality as a symphony of overlapping frequencies. One thought leads to five others. One emotion opens a portal. One sensory trigger shifts the entire channel. It's not disorder. It's multidimensional processing.

That's why you might walk into a room and forget why you came in — not because you're broken, but because you dropped the frequency you were holding. You didn't lose the thought. You just lost the signal.

Understanding memory as frequency — not storage — reframes everything. Forgetfulness becomes fluctuation. Creativity becomes connectivity. Healing becomes re-tuning.

Collective memory also exists in this field. That's why people across time can access similar myths, ideas, or inventions — because they're tuning into the same informational stream.

And the more awareness you bring to how you interact with the Field, the more skillfully you can access it.

Because this isn't just about memory. It's about timelines. And that's where we go next.

Time Is a Coordinate, Not a Line

Time isn't a line — it's a grid. Each moment is a coordinate point in the quantum field, and consciousness is the cursor that selects which version you enter.

Linear time is a construct your avatar uses to organize experience in this dimension. But at a higher level of awareness, time is not a straight path — it's a layered map of possibilities, all existing simultaneously. Physicists call this the "block universe" theory — the idea that past, present, and future already exist, and time doesn't flow but is simply experienced differently depending on your position of observation. What you call "past" and "future" are simply different coordinates in the quantum field, waiting for your consciousness to tune into them.

According to quantum theory, the concept of superposition explains how particles can exist in multiple states at once — until one is observed. In much the same way, your potential realities exist in a field of probability until your consciousness locks onto one. Observation collapses potential into form, and your focus determines which version of reality loads.

Time isn't a straight line — it's more like a cosmic choose-your-own-adventure book. At every moment, you're choosing which page to turn to based on your frequency. And unlike those 90s paperbacks, you can't just peek ahead to cheat the ending. You don't flip the pages with your hands — you flip them with your vibration. Each emotional state bookmarks a different outcome.

This is why healing your past now creates a new future. You're not erasing what happened — you're shifting the version of yourself that experienced it. You're tuning into a storyline where your pain becomes wisdom and your wounds no longer run the plot. That version of you — the healed one — already exists in a parallel timeline. You're not forcing a new future. You're jumping to the version that remembers who they became on the other side of it.

You're not moving through time like a train on a track. You're jumping timelines — moment to moment — based on the frequency you carry.

The only real moment is now. It's the portal through which all realities are accessed. So if you want to switch endings, change your frequency and flip to the next chapter.

That's also why the frequency you're tuned into directly impacts what version of time you experience. At one level, it determines the emotional and perceptual lens through which you view events. Two people can live through the same year or moment in history and have radically different realities — because their beliefs, wounds, and awareness shape how time renders for them.

On a soul level, the frequency you carry may resonate with the vibe of a specific time period. You chose to enter the game during a chapter that matched your mission.

When and where you were born isn't just chance. It's part of the setup. Think of it like selecting your player settings: year, environment, difficulty mode, supporting cast, and quest objectives. Your birth wasn't random. It was a strategic login to the perfect level for your mission. The culture, technology, and challenges of your era create a backdrop that's meant to help you learn something specific. Some mystics and quantum biologists suggest your DNA acts like a tuning fork, resonating with the vibrational signature of the era you're born into — syncing your soul's lessons with the timeline best suited for them. Your life unfolds within that setting, but the way you experience it — the lens you bring — is uniquely yours. That combination creates your personal version of the Remembrance Game.

Time also moves in cycles — both personally and collectively. These cycles influence the themes, emotions, and events that rise to the surface in every era. Think of collective consciousness like the weather system of the Remembrance Game. In the Dark Ages, the collective was thick with fear, control, and survival. In today's Age of Aquarius, we have access to more information, awareness, and potential than ever before. Each cycle brings its own invitations, initiations, and gifts. These cycles are like seasons in the simulation — each one bringing new lessons, upgrades, and weather patterns to evolve through.

Astrology is one way we can track these larger energetic tides. Planetary alignments influence the mood, lessons, and themes that shape the collective consciousness. While everyone feels these waves, how they experience them depends on their personal frequency, beliefs, and emotions — kind of like how two people can hear the same song but have completely different reactions depending on their vibe.

You are part of this cycle — not just watching it, but helping shape it. Your perspective, your healing, and your choices ripple through the collective field.

And that's what makes you so significant.

You are a once-in-all-of-existence frequency. There has never been another version of Source with your exact lens, timing, gifts, and blueprint. That's why your experience is sacred. Because you are Source — in a form it has never taken before.

And every moment you live is a line in its story of remembrance.

Reality is not solid — it's a touchable, virtual-reality hologram. A vibrational projection rendered from a quantum field. What feels like matter is just slowed-down light. What looks like permanence is just code holding its form until your consciousness shifts. You're not just walking through time — you're moving through a grid. And every moment you change your frequency, the entire structure reorients around you. A new version loads. A new level of the game becomes available. You didn't go somewhere new — you tuned into it.

The Rules of the Game

Just like every game has mechanics and built-in rules, the
Remembrance Game comes with its own set of operating laws —
some flexible, some foundational.

There are default settings in the simulation — like gravity, aging, and
decay — that appear solid because almost everyone agrees on them.
These shared experiences give the game structure, like the physics
engine in a video game. But are they truly fixed? Or are they just
collective beliefs coded so deeply into the system that they feel
unchangeable at our current level of awareness?

Some elements, like polarity and contrast, seem to be core
mechanics of the Remembrance Game. These serve a greater
purpose — providing the tension and contrast that fuels soul growth.
Still, even these express themselves differently depending on your
alignment and consciousness.

Then there are fixed spiritual laws — what you might call the
universal programming language of this reality. These laws operate
at every level of the simulation, no matter your beliefs. They're not
based on cultural systems or temporary programming. They're part
of the engine itself.

These are not moral rules or religious commandments. They're
energetic laws — constants that govern how the simulation
functions, regardless of personal beliefs or cultural background.

Rooted in Hermetic philosophy and echoed in metaphysical teachings across time, these laws form the underlying code of how reality operates.

But before we dive into the twelve laws, let's unlock the master key behind them all...

The Law Beneath the Game: Mentalism

Before we explore the Universal Laws that shape this reality, there's one master key you need to know — **the Law of Mentalism**. This principle, drawn from ancient Hermetic wisdom, teaches that **all is mind**. Reality is not something happening to you — it's something being projected *through* you. Every law, every pattern, every reflection in your external world is first filtered through the internal screen of your consciousness. Your beliefs form the blueprint. Your thoughts generate the code. Your emotional energy powers the system. The game you're playing is a mental simulation, and **your mind is the command center**. Everything that appears around you is responding to what's running within you.

This law sets the foundation for the others that follow. The 12 Universal Laws are like the game's operating rules — but **Mentalism is the engine that renders the simulation itself**.

These are the 12 Universal Laws that influence your experience in the Remembrance Game:

1. **Law of Divine Oneness**: Everything is connected. Every thought, action, and intention ripples through the collective.

2. **Law of Vibration**: Everything vibrates. Your frequency determines the quality of what you attract and how the simulation responds.

3. **Law of Correspondence**: Your outer reality mirrors your inner beliefs and state of consciousness.

4. **Law of Attraction**: Like attracts like. Your energy — not your words — draws experiences to you.

5. **Law of Inspired Action**: Movement is required. Taking aligned steps bridges intention and manifestation.

6. **Law of Perpetual Transmutation of Energy**: Energy is always moving. Higher vibrations can transform lower ones.

7. **Law of Cause and Effect**: Every action has a reaction. Energy in = energy out.

8. **Law of Compensation**: You receive what you energetically earn — not always when or how you expect.

9. **Law of Relativity**: All experience is relative. Challenges help you see contrast and develop strength.

10. **Law of Polarity**: Everything has an opposite. Contrast brings clarity and fuels expansion.

11. **Law of Rhythm**: Life moves in cycles. Trust the rise and fall. Nothing is stagnant.

12. **Law of Gender**: Masculine and feminine energies exist in all things. Creation flows from balance.

Beliefs, trauma, and programming act like filters over the code. But so do love, trust, and faith. That's why one person can experience a miracle while another sees limitation. It's not just biology or chance — it's vibration and belief alignment.

That's also why major shifts — emotional breakthroughs, deep forgiveness, or true presence — can change your physical reality. Because the simulation doesn't just listen to what you want. It renders based on who you've become.

Not the mask you wear or the words you say — but the vibration you embody when no one's watching. The universe doesn't care how beautiful your vision board is if your energy is still stuck in doomscroll mode and self-doubt. You can't chant affirmations over chaos and expect miracles. The field reads your vibe — not your Pinterest.

That's not to say vision boards don't work. They absolutely can be powerful tools to help clarify your desires, set intentions, and even begin rewiring your brain to support a new version of you. But you can't just make a collage and wait. You have to **embody** it. If you paint a few pictures but don't start seeing yourself as an artist, you'll never feel like one. Being comes before becoming. You have to walk like it, talk like it, and live like it before the simulation renders that identity back to you.

And if you're going to play the game, you might as well learn how to play it well. Or at least stop rage-quitting every time life doesn't go as planned.

Even the best players hit restart more than once before they mastered the game. That's part of the process.

The good news? You're not stuck. You're not broken. You're just learning how to read the code — and the more you align your inner world with the laws of the game, the more effortlessly your external world updates.

And since time doesn't actually exist, the universe isn't keeping score or judging how long it takes you to repeat a level. You'll keep looping that level until you integrate the lesson — and the moment you do, a new version of the Game loads.

Shift the code. Change the game.

Reflection Prompt

- Think back to a time when a belief or expectation you held seemed to shape the outcome of a situation — like expecting criticism and then receiving cold feedback. What does that teach you about the 'rules' governing your experience?
- Have you ever lost track of time doing something you love, or watched the clock tick painfully during a tough conversation? What did that reveal about your relationship with time?
- Describe a recent moment when you noticed a subtle nudge — an intuitive hit or a synchronicity that felt like the simulation giving you a signal. What do you think it was trying to show you?

Next Level: The Avatar – Who You Think You Are vs. Who's Actually Playing

In the next chapter, we'll shift from the outer field to your inner interface. Because you're not just observing the simulation — you're navigating it through a character. One with preloaded traits, behaviors, reactions, and subconscious scripts.

This avatar was built for this game. But if you don't know where the controls are, you'll keep reacting from its defaults instead of rewriting the code.

So the question becomes:

Are you playing the avatar — or is it playing you?

CHAPTER 4: THE AVATAR – WHO YOU THINK YOU ARE VS. WHO'S ACTUALLY PLAYING

This is where the Game gets personal.

In every simulation, there's a player and a playable character. In your case, that character is the version of you that you've come to identify with — your name, your body, your job, your history, your likes and dislikes. The personality you think is "you." That's your avatar. But the one actually playing? That's a whole other story.

Quick Definitions:

- **Avatar** = The character you play in this lifetime (body, personality, identity)
- **Player** = Your higher self or soul, guiding the avatar through the game

Your avatar is the expression your higher consciousness uses to interact with the simulation. It's your unique skin in the simulation — custom-coded with specific traits, challenges, karma, and preferences. But here's the kicker: most people forget they're the player. They get so identified with the avatar that they start thinking the game is happening *to* them instead of *through* them.

Forgetting who you really are? That's not a glitch — it's part of the design.

Your simulation character comes with filters, scripts, and programming inherited from family, culture, and early life. It's like booting up a character mid-story, with someone else's script already running — and no memory of how it got there. You don't remember creating it, but now you're living it.

So the question becomes: are you playing the avatar... or is the avatar playing you?

In this chapter, we'll decode the avatar system — how your mind, emotions, nervous system, and subconscious beliefs shape your character's default behaviors, and how to spot when autopilot programming takes over — and how to reclaim the controls so the real you (the one behind the eyes) can start driving again.

Because only when the Player remembers they're the one holding the controller can the avatar finally evolve beyond its code.

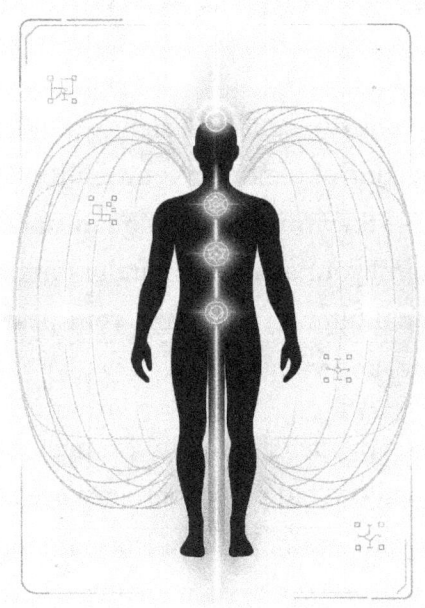

Avatar Hardware
The Physical & Energetic Body

Avatar Vessel – The Physical Shell

Your avatar isn't just a clunky human costume — it's a marvel of biological design. Imagine a super advanced, biologically engineered VR suit. Your senses are the input interface, converting signals from the Field into experience. But the real magic? This suit is self-healing, regenerating, adapting, and even capable of replicating itself. You are, quite literally, walking around in a living miracle — one of the most sophisticated organic technologies Source has ever dreamed into being.

Avatar Input System – Senses, Perception & Filters

In this simulation, your five senses — sight, sound, touch, taste, and smell — act like the control panel for your reality. They don't show you *objective truth* — they translate raw quantum data into something meaningful your avatar can understand. But they do this through your personal filters: your brain, your past experiences, your emotional state, and your beliefs.

And here's the twist: you never actually see, hear, taste, touch, or smell *anything* directly. What you experience are electrical signals being processed by your brain. Your sensory organs collect data, convert it to impulses, and your brain creates a high-def, fully immersive movie that you call "real life." Wild, right?

And it gets even trickier — your avatar doesn't read all that input equally. Your brain is constantly tuning out what it thinks is unimportant. Neuroscience calls this *interoception* — your brain's ability to filter and interpret internal bodily signals. It prioritizes what it thinks is relevant to your survival, which is why deeper signals — like intuition or subtle energy — often get ignored when you're stuck in stress mode. That's also why you can stop noticing a bad smell after a few minutes or forget you're wearing socks until someone mentions them. It's called sensory adaptation, and it's your system's way of avoiding overload.

But here's where the real magic (and mischief) happens:

What you don't focus on, you miss.

Ever eaten while scrolling your phone and suddenly realized you didn't even *taste* your food? You missed the warmth of the bite, the crunch, the richness — because your awareness was elsewhere. And if we can miss something as basic as flavor, imagine what we're not picking up in the emotional, intuitive, or energetic layers of reality.

You're not just perceiving reality — you're perceiving a filtered, customized, priority-based version of reality. Kind of like your brain is the executive producer of your life's reality show, constantly editing footage to fit the plot it thinks you're living.

And the more present you become, the more access you gain. The game gets richer. The feedback sharper. The experiences deeper.

So the next time you're enjoying chocolate or soaking up sunlight, pause and remember: your avatar isn't just reacting — it's interpreting. And you're the one deciding what gets through the filter.

But physical perception is only half the story. Your avatar isn't just receiving data — it's broadcasting it too. It's also reading and transmitting energy at every moment.

Avatar Energy System – Regulate, Receive & Broadcast

Your avatar isn't just flesh and bone — it's an integrated biological and energetic interface designed to receive, process, and transmit frequency. Every component — your nervous system, glands, chakras, emotions, and perception — plays a role in how you experience and influence reality.

These systems don't just respond to your environment — they interact with the code of the Game. They're tools your higher self uses to tune into insight and broadcast intention.

Together, these systems form your energetic interface:

- ⚡ **Regulator & Stabilizer:** Nervous system – anchors your ability to hold frequency.

- 🗒 **Receiver & Tuner:** Pineal gland – anchors your connection to higher insight.

- 💚 **Broadcaster & Resonance Anchor:** Heart + Chakras – anchor the emotional frequency you send into the Field.
  Each one influences how clearly you experience the Game — and how powerfully you shape it.

Let's start with the foundation: your **nervous system**. It's the regulator. The anchor that determines how well your avatar can stay connected to its signal.

The nervous system isn't just a biological system — it's the body's frequency regulator. When your system is dysregulated, it's harder to hear your intuition, access clarity, or shift your code.
Regulating your system brings you back to your baseline signal — the version of you that can consciously reprogram the game.

Once your nervous system is stabilized, it unlocks the next tier of your energetic interface. Think of it like leveling up — your signal gets stronger, your tools come online, and the higher guidance becomes easier to decode.

Let's start with the **pineal gland** — often called your **Wi-Fi receiver** to higher dimensions. This small, pinecone-shaped gland sits at the center of your brain and plays a crucial role in bridging physical and energetic perception. In ancient spiritual traditions, it's associated with the **third eye** — a gateway to higher awareness and multidimensional insight. Scientifically, it helps regulate your circadian rhythm, but energetically, it's believed to assist with intuition, spiritual downloads, and non-physical navigation.

When your pineal gland is clear, you can receive intuitive insight and stay connected to your higher self. But many people's "receivers" get blocked — by trauma, fluoride, overstimulation, or disconnection from nature — making it harder to perceive subtle frequencies. And just as the pineal gland helps you tune inward and receive subtle signals, your heart helps you broadcast those signals outward — shaping the energetic imprint you leave on the world around you.

The heart is far more than just a physical organ. It's the electromagnetic powerhouse of your avatar. The heart generates a torus field 60 times greater in amplitude than the brain's and can be detected several feet away. According to the HeartMath Institute, this field responds in real time to your emotional state, broadcasting coherence or chaos into your environment — and syncing with the fields of others.

But the heart isn't just a transmitter — it's also a center of intelligence. It has its own neural network, often called the 'heart brain,' which processes information independently from your cranial brain. This means the heart doesn't just feel — it *knows*. Heart-based intelligence guides you in making aligned decisions, accessing intuition, and feeling a sense of inner harmony. When your heart is in coherence, it creates resonance across your entire system — supporting emotional regulation, physical vitality, and clearer access to your higher guidance.

In many ways, your heart is your energetic anchor. It's not only the bridge between your lower and upper chakras, but between your human self and your higher self.

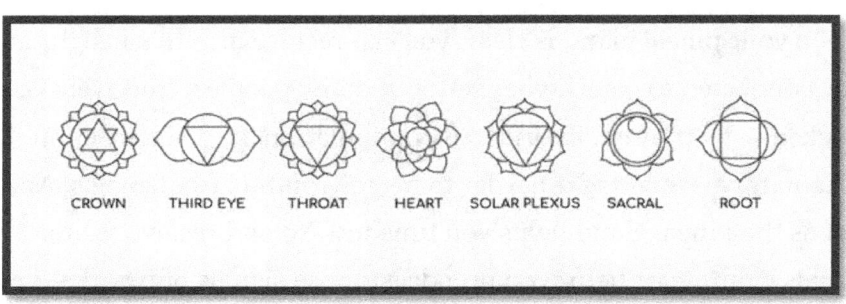

CROWN   THIRD EYE   THROAT   HEART   SOLAR PLEXUS   SACRAL   ROOT

Then there are the **chakras** — seven primary energy centers running down the middle of your body. Each one aligns with a specific layer of your human experience — from survival and intimacy to intuition and divine connection. From root to crown, they govern core themes: survival, pleasure, willpower, love, expression, intuition, and connection to the divine.

Chakras act like data routers — translating, transmitting, and modulating energetic input and output. They also contribute to your energetic broadcast — each center expressing its own frequency depending on how open, balanced, or blocked it is. While the heart field creates the overarching resonance, the chakras refine and channel that signal. When open and aligned, your avatar functions smoothly across all systems. When blocked or out of sync, you may feel stuck, reactive, or disoriented.

To keep your avatar's energy system clear, tuned, and fully operational, it's essential to support all three layers: **regulation** (nervous system), **reception** (pineal gland), and **broadcasting + modulation** (heart field and chakras).

Practices like meditation, visualization, clean eating, sun-gazing, breathwork, and energy healing modalities like Reiki can help you maintain balance, alignment, and flow. These tools act like system upgrades — strengthening your avatar's ability to receive intuitive downloads, regulate emotional frequency, and transmit a coherent signal into the Field.

Studies have shown that emotional coherence — especially heart-brain coherence — can increase intuition, reduce stress, and improve cognitive function, making your avatar more effective in every area of the Game.

Your avatar isn't just reacting to the world — it's co-creating with it. And the more consciously you work with these systems, the more empowered you become to navigate the Game like a master — with clarity, coherence, and creative control.

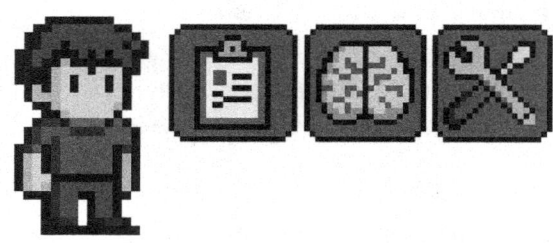

Avatar Software
The Inner Code & Conditioning

🎮 Avatar Profile

Much like a video game character, your avatar comes with a unique player profile — a pre-loaded set of attributes, stats, and conditions chosen before entry. This includes your date and place of birth, biological gender, gender identity, sexual orientation, family dynamics, religious upbringing, socioeconomic class, and even inherited trauma. Some avatars spawn into the game with additional layers, like chronic illness, mental health conditions, or neurodivergent wiring. These aren't glitches — they're quests. They shape your perception, your obstacles, and your potential gifts.

You could think of these traits like the sliders and toggles you'd adjust while building a character in a game. They don't define your essence, but they do impact your experience, adding both richness and resistance. These aren't punishments — they're starting conditions, designed to shape your arc of evolution.

Developmental Phases — From Programmed to Player

Your avatar doesn't go from asleep to awakened overnight. There's a natural progression — a set of phases where your awareness and ability to consciously play the Game gradually evolve. Each phase is marked by shifts in brainwave patterns, belief systems, and identity development.

Level 1: Ages 0–7 — Absorption Mode (Theta Brainwaves)
- In this stage, your brain operates mostly in **theta waves** — a hypnotic state ideal for subconscious programming.
- You absorb everything: beliefs, emotional patterns, societal roles, and family dynamics. This becomes the baseline code your avatar will run by default.

Level 2: Ages 8–14 — Imitation Mode (Alpha Brainwaves)
- You begin mimicking the world around you. Seeking identity through school, peers, and culture.
- The avatar's early scripts are reinforced or challenged, but still largely unquestioned.

Level 3: Ages 15–29 – Simulation Buy-In (Beta Brainwaves)

- You fully buy into the simulation. Chase achievement, identity, success, and external validation.
- Often the most programmed phase. Many people get stuck here.

Level 4: Ages 30–42 – Awakening & Deprogramming

- Life begins to show you where the scripts don't work. You begin questioning who you really are.
- Pain, burnout, or major life events often trigger a shift.

Level 5: Ages 42+ – Player Mode Activation

- You begin to trust the Player. Less reaction, more response. Less programming, more presence.
- You start designing your reality consciously, shedding roles and aligning with purpose.

This isn't a rigid formula — it's a flexible framework. Some awaken earlier, others later. Some revisit stages in cycles. But recognizing the arc helps you see where you are and what's unfolding.

No phase is wrong. But the Player is always inviting you to go deeper.

🎭 Avatar Archetypes – The Roles We Default To

Before we dive into the deeper programming, let's look at some of the common "default roles" that avatars tend to adopt based on their early coding. These aren't good or bad — they're just survival patterns your avatar chose to stay safe or be seen.

The Achiever

Feels only as worthy as their latest accomplishment.

The Caretaker

Gains value by tending to everyone else's needs.

The Outsider

Always on the edge, observing but never belonging.

The Fixer

Feels responsible for making everything okay for others.

The Rebel

Defines self by rejecting structure, rules, or authority.

The Chameleon

Adapts constantly to match the room, losing sense of self.

Recognizing your archetype helps you decode the script you've been running. It also softens the shame. You weren't "broken" — you were brilliant enough to survive.

Ego Scripts in the Simulation:

- "You'll fail if you try that."
- "You have to be perfect to be loved."
- "Who do you think you are?"
- "Better not change — at least you know how to survive this."

And once you see the role, you can choose whether you want to keep playing it.

🆘 Ego: Autopilot and Survival Mode

From the moment you enter the simulation, your avatar starts absorbing data — family rules, school systems, social norms, and unspoken expectations. These layers form the "mask" your avatar learns to wear: who you think you need to be in order to stay safe, accepted, or successful.

Beneath all this sits the **ego** — your avatar's internal narrator and self-protection system. The ego isn't evil. It's the part of your programming built to keep you safe, to organize the world into categories, and to help you function in the simulation. The ego functions like an internal alert system — always scanning for potential threats based on past experiences. It's designed to protect you, not punish you. But the ego is also reactive, rigid, and fear-driven. It builds identities out of survival, not truth. It craves control, certainty, and familiarity. It will even lie to you to keep you in what's known — because the unknown feels dangerous.

The ego acts as the avatar's autopilot. And when you're unaware of it, it drives the show. It keeps running loops from the past.

According to Polyvagal Theory, many of your automatic behaviors — like fight, flight, freeze, or fawn (people-pleasing) — aren't flaws in your character, but protective reflexes hardwired into your nervous system to help you survive perceived danger. The ego wears masks that helped you survive — but now keep you from thriving.

Beneath the ego's defenses lives an even deeper layer of software — your emotional code — a blueprint of patterns, fears, attachments, and beliefs that often runs without your awareness. In cognitive psychology, these are known as core beliefs — unconscious assumptions formed in early life that shape how you interpret yourself and the world. Many of these beliefs stem from early attachment dynamics, where your nervous system learned how to stay safe and connected in your specific environment. This code is largely written in your first seven years, during the theta brainwave stage of development. This foundation acts like an operating system — automating your behaviors, reactions, and emotional responses, even long after the original circumstances have passed.

And just like buggy code in a game, these patterns can keep you stuck. They replay old stories, recreate familiar conflicts, and trap you in identity loops that no longer serve your evolution.

But there's a hack: **awareness**.

When the Player becomes aware of the ego and the emotional code instead of reacting from them, it can begin to rewrite the system. That's where real freedom begins — not by fighting the avatar, but by understanding how it was built and reclaiming the controller. Once you see the code, you can change the game.

And the next step? Learning how to recode it — intentionally, energetically, and in alignment with your Player.

First, the **ego**. This is your avatar's internal narrator and built-in safety mechanism. The ego isn't evil. It's the part of the avatar designed to keep you safe. It constructs identities, enforces labels, and sets boundaries — all based on past programming. But while it can be helpful for navigating the 3D world, it often runs on outdated fear-based code. That's when the ego stops being a map and starts becoming a cage.

The ego wants certainty. It wants to control the narrative. Because it filters everything through the lens of survival, it often sees discomfort or uncertainty as danger — even when you're no longer at risk. It will even lie to you to keep you within known limits — because it associates safety with familiarity, not with truth.

When you begin operating from your Player state, the ego doesn't disappear — but it no longer runs the show. You can thank it, love it, and gently set it in the passenger seat while your higher self drives. The ego isn't the enemy — it's just not meant to be the engineer of your evolution. And when left unchecked, it becomes the autopilot program running your life — repeating old scripts even when they no longer serve your growth. Thankfully, your brain isn't fixed in place. Through *neuroplasticity* — your brain's ability to rewire itself — you can create new patterns, shift old beliefs, and respond from a place of presence rather than programming.

🔓 Unlocking Your Code – Tools to Decode Your Avatar

There are also ancient and modern tools that can help you understand the default settings of your avatar — tools like astrology, numerology, Human Design, and Gene Keys. These frameworks offer insight into your natural tendencies, life themes, energetic blueprint, and even karmic patterns. You can start by pulling your free natal chart, running your Human Design bodygraph, or checking your life path number — many of these tools are freely available and easy to explore. They're not meant to limit you, but to give you clues about your unique wiring and purpose in this lifetime.

What These Tools Can Reveal

- **Astrology** – Life themes, emotional patterns, cycles
- **Human Design** – Energy mechanics, decision-making strategy
- **Gene Keys** – Shadow patterns, soul evolution
- **Numerology** – Core purpose, frequency of your name and birthdate

Exploring these systems is like reading the game manual your avatar came with. You don't have to believe every detail, but they can spark self-awareness and help you decode aspects of your avatar you've always felt but never had words for. Even if you approach them with curiosity instead of certainty, they can reveal insights that resonate deeply or challenge you to see yourself through a new lens.

Later in the book, we'll introduce a Map of Consciousness — a chart of awareness levels that helps you read both your inner states and the energies around you. Think of it as the Game's dashboard, showing you which "level" of vibration you and your environment are operating on so you can tune your signal and navigate with precision.

Signs You're in Avatar Mode vs. Player Mode

It's not always obvious who's driving. But here are a few clues:

Avatar Mode	Player Mode
Reactive & defensive	Observant & responsive
Loops in old patterns	Sees patterns as lessons
Seeks external validation	Moves from inner truth
Feels like life happens to them	Remembers life happens through them
Controlled by fear	Guided by curiosity

Recognizing these shifts is half the battle. Once you know who's holding the controller, you can start changing the moves you make.

If you're not sure whether you're in avatar mode, just check your inner monologue. If it sounds like a dramatic soap opera or your 9th grade math teacher, congrats — you're not the one holding the controller.

🦴 Rewiring Your Avatar

Once you start recognizing when your avatar is running the show, you can begin shifting how it operates — from default programming to intentional design. This is where transformation happens — not by forcing yourself to "be better," but by updating the code your avatar is running on.

Rewiring doesn't mean becoming someone else. It means clearing the static from the signal so your true frequency can transmit with clarity.

There are many ways to update the code:

- **Awareness + reflection**: Noticing a pattern is the first step to shifting it.
- **Stillness + meditation**: When you pause, you disrupt the loop. Silence creates the space for the Player to speak.
- **Breathwork**: Conscious breathing regulates your nervous system, helps release stuck energy, and returns you to presence.
- **Somatic tools**: Your body holds memories. Movement, breath, and nervous system regulation help dissolve stuck emotional energy.
- **Energy healing**: Modalities like Reiki help clear energetic blocks in the field.
- **Subconscious reprogramming**: Practices like hypnosis, inner child work, and Quantum Reprogramming™ can help recode beliefs from the root.
- **Aligned action**: Each time you choose a new response, you're laying neural pathways that support your future self.

Every new action reinforces neural pathways through neuroplasticity — your brain's ability to rewire itself based on conscious repetition and emotional engagement.

And just like that, you're not just playing the game — you're rewriting it.

💔 The Pain and Purpose of the Avatar

One of the hardest things to accept in this simulation is that growth often hurts. Just like a child being born or a seed pushing through soil, expansion comes with pressure and discomfort. Pain is part of the avatar experience — not because you're doing something wrong, but because you're evolving.

The avatar is wired for survival. When its comfort zones are threatened, it reacts with fear, resistance, or shutdown. But from the Player's perspective, those moments are portals — not punishments. Pain is a prompt from the simulation — it gets your attention when your current code no longer aligns with your soul's direction. It reroutes you. It shows you where your programming is ready to evolve.

Some avatars are born with more intense challenges: chronic pain, trauma, illness, or neurodivergence. These aren't defects. They're advanced quests — coded with complexity to unlock deeper empathy, resilience, and soul remembrance.

You are not your avatar's pain. But you are here to work with it. To alchemize it. To let it refine you, not define you.

Reflection Prompt

- What's a "mask" you've worn to stay safe, fit in, or be accepted?
- How do you tend to show up when you're in avatar mode?
- Where can you surrender and let the Player drive?

Next Level: Game Features – How the Simulation Was Customized for You

In the next chapter, we'll explore how your simulation wasn't randomly generated — it was precisely tailored. From your birth circumstances and body to your timeline, karma, and life quests, every feature was selected to help you grow through experience. Think of it as the customization screen before entering the game: the variables you chose to help unlock the next level of remembrance.

CHAPTER 5:
GAME FEATURES – HOW THE SIMULATION WAS CUSTOMIZED FOR YOU

What if your life isn't random?
What if the challenges, relationships, even your birthday, are all settings you chose before the game began?

This chapter explores the built-in features of your simulation experience — the spiritual source code — preset variables that influence your avatar's settings from the very beginning. These features include who you were born to, where you were born, the level of karma you're carrying, your soul's mission, and the optional side quests you get to explore along the way.

The Higher Self: The Player Behind the Player

You, as the avatar, are not the one in control of the game. The one truly navigating the journey is your **Higher Self** — the Player behind the Avatar.

Your Higher Self sees the full map, holds your soul mission, and manages the **master control panel** of your experience. It's not just there to whisper life advice during meditations. It operates like divine air traffic control — coordinating emotional cues, synchronicities, surprise plot twists, and even the timing of when you run into that person you "randomly" meet three times in one week.

Think of it as your personal frequency-based GPS system. If you're veering off-path, it reroutes you. Ignore enough signs, and you won't get punished — but you might get hit with a full system reboot: a breakdown, breakup, or spontaneous career implosion.

And it's not only managing your timeline — it's syncing yours with others. That job rejection? A setup for a better offer. That heartbreak? A portal into your next mission. The Higher Self is orchestrating a multi-dimensional chessboard that involves people, places, and opportunities far beyond what your avatar can comprehend in the moment.

Every job loss, every love interest, every intuitive nudge and every perfectly-timed delay is part of the plan. You're not making it up. You're being guided.

So, if life feels weirdly specific right now — it probably is.

The Higher Self isn't punishing you. It's redirecting you toward alignment. Think of it like the control room in *Inside Out* — but instead of Joy and Sadness arguing over buttons, it's your Higher Self calmly adjusting the sliders on emotion, timing, and who enters your scene. You might not see the full dashboard, but trust — it's running the show behind the curtain. And it won't stop nudging until you remember who you are. You chose this configuration. The settings were customized for what your soul came to master.

Starter Pack: Parents and Lineage

Yes, your soul chose your parents.
Not because they'd be perfect — but because they'd give you the **perfect conditions** for growth.

Your family of origin sets the stage for early wounding, gifts, and karmic themes. Whether you were born into trauma or love (or both), it was chosen to activate the experiences your soul wanted to master.

This choice also connects you to a **lineage** — your ancestral line and everything it carries: programming, blessings, pain, and patterns. Research in epigenetics even shows that trauma can be biologically passed down — meaning your healing doesn't just help you, it sends a ripple back through your lineage. Your mission: Heal what they couldn't. Carry forward what still serves.

Think of it like choosing the starter pack for a video game. Maybe you got the Emotional Chaos Bundle — complete with abandonment issues and a few bonus triggers. Or maybe you signed up for high expectations from a well-meaning perfectionist. Either way, it wasn't random.

Souls often choose intense families not as punishment, but because those environments create pressure — and pressure forms the diamond. It pushes you to grow, question, transform, and ultimately rise.

You may have felt dropped into a storyline you never would've chosen in your right mind. But you weren't in your mind — you were in your soul. And your soul knew what it was doing.

After all, if souls played video games, would they really pick the predictable ones? Or would they dive into the ones with the biggest twists, deepest challenges, and the greatest chance to level up?

Game Coordinates: Birth Time and Place

When and where you were born is not random. These are the **game stage and coordinates** for your simulation.

- Your **birthplace** sets the stage for cultural conditioning, environmental programming, and available opportunities.

- Your **birthdate and time** set the coordinates of your level — locking in your astrological blueprint, collective influences, and divine timing.

All of these shape your avatar's base stats, so to speak.

And it goes deeper. Your **date of birth** doesn't just impact your personal astrology — it also locks you into the timeline of the collective consciousness. In other words, your soul didn't just choose your personal life — it chose the collective storyline you'd be a part of. It's like loading into a specific "game patch" — one filled with global events, energetic weather, and cultural scripts already in motion.

Born in the middle of a revolution? That fire may live in you. Born during a tech boom? You might be coded to innovate.

Your soul knew exactly when to enter. Because timing isn't just divine — it's strategic. Psychologist Viktor Frankl wrote that purpose is often born from suffering — that meaning arises not in the absence of struggle, but through transcending it. Souls often choose pressure not for punishment, but for purpose.

Difficulty Settings: How Karma Shapes the Game

Every player enters the Game with a different challenge rating. Your karma sets the **difficulty level** of your simulation — like choosing whether you're starting a game on beginner, intermediate, or expert mode.

Some souls opt into "easy mode" — with peaceful homes, supportive environments, and minimal trauma. Others load into the simulation on "expert mode" — complete with generational baggage, intense life lessons, and soul-level missions that demand deep healing and growth.

But this isn't about fairness. It's about functionality. The more karma you're carrying — whether from past lives, ancestral patterns, or soul agreements — the more potential you've set yourself up to unlock. Think of karma as energetic weight. The heavier it is, the more spiritual strength and resilience you build by lifting it.

This sets the initial parameters of your simulation. Just like a challenging level in a game makes you learn faster, adapt quicker, and master new skills, your karmic setting forces you to evolve — and gives you more opportunities to activate your purpose.

And the best part? Your difficulty level isn't fixed. Your **actions** — your integrity, healing, and awareness — are what rebalance the game in your favor. It's not punishment. It's progress tracking.

Karma doesn't just shape your path — it codes the level you're playing.

If you enter the game with karma from past lives or generational patterns, your simulation might start on "hard mode." That means more obstacles, more triggering people, and more opportunities to earn strength points by choosing love over fear.

Your **actions** are what upgrade your karma score. Lie, cheat, or manipulate? Expect to face bosses who mirror those traits back to you. That's not punishment — it's a coded feedback loop. This mirrors how your brain forms beliefs through repetition and emotional impact — what you reinforce becomes the reality you experience. But choose honesty, compassion, and integrity, and the level recalibrates. New paths open. Helpers show up. Challenges become checkpoints, not roadblocks.

There's an old saying: what you send out comes back threefold. In the Game of Remembrance, that's a karma multiplier. What you give — through thoughts, words, and especially **actions** — returns amplified.

So if your current level feels stacked with hardship or toxic characters, don't just ask, "Why is this happening?" Ask, "What am I still broadcasting?" and "What can I choose differently now?"

Because every time you shift your karma through conscious action, you don't just make the level easier.
You level up your avatar.
You strengthen your soul.
And the Game always responds to your signal.

Here are a few real-world examples of how karmic coding plays out in the Game:

Karma in Action: How the Game Responds to Your Moves

Karma Glitch: Gossip attracts drama.
Karma Upgrade: Forgiveness unlocks emotional freedom.
Karma Glitch: Trying to skip lessons usually unlocks harder ones.
Karma Upgrade: Helping others triggers surprise rewards.
Karma Glitch: Manipulating people leads to chaotic characters.
Karma Upgrade: Speaking truth invites aligned relationships.

Game Tip: Karma loads the difficulty level. Your actions will lower or increase the challenge.

Main Quests: Your Soul's Core Missions

Every soul enters with a **primary mission** — core lessons it came to master in this lifetime. This mission is written into your code before you ever take your first breath. It's not assigned as punishment — it's chosen as a path to evolution.

These missions can look different for everyone. For some, it's learning unconditional love. For others, it's reclaiming their voice, breaking generational cycles, healing from trauma, embodying self-worth, or becoming a teacher or guide for others — and for some strong souls, all of the above.

Your mission often hides in plain sight — it shows up in the themes that repeat, the areas where you struggle most, or the things that ignite your passion or pain. That's not a flaw in the system — it's how your Higher Self flags the levels you're here to master. Where there's friction, there's potential.

And your soul mission doesn't need to be flashy or famous. Not everyone is here to lead revolutions or write bestsellers. Some are here to love deeply, raise conscious children, or heal their lineage silently through presence and integrity.

There's no such thing as a small mission when it's chosen by the soul.

And the beautiful part? You're never off it. Even detours, breakdowns, and rest phases are part of your unique soul curriculum. You can't miss your mission — you can only delay it by forgetting your power. But even then, the Game gently nudges you back toward the remembering.

Side Quests: Optional Paths with Hidden Rewards

But along the way, there are **side quests** — the hobbies, relationships, talents, creative callings, and unexpected adventures that enrich your game and expand your frequency. These aren't detours. They're power-ups. Psychologists call this *intrinsic motivation* — activities you do for joy, not outcome. These experiences naturally elevate your state of being and promote neurochemical balance, which energetically upgrades your gameplay.

Think of a side quest as anything that lights you up. Starting a garden. Writing poetry. Dancing under the stars. Launching a weird little Etsy shop that makes you smile. These are soul-expanding experiences that shift your vibration, attract aligned people, and open new levels you didn't even know were coded into your timeline.

And sometimes a side quest turns into your main quest. That's the magic of following joy.

So if you've ever felt like you're "behind" or off-track, remember: you're not stuck — you might just be in a side quest that's unlocking tools for your next evolution. Either way, the Game is always giving you something valuable — whether it looks like progress, play, or even rest.

Custom-Coded:
You're Not Broken — You're Built for This

Everything you've lived is part of the custom coding that makes your simulation unique.

The family that hurt you? Was part of the code.
The city you grew up in? Loaded your early levels.
The desire to write, dance, or speak? That's a mission marker.
You're not behind. You're not off-course. And you're definitely not broken..

Your avatar was designed with precision — complete with strengths, sensitivities, and stretch points. Even the glitches, breakdowns, and meltdowns are part of your calibration. In software terms, this is like running a stress test — not to break the system, but to reveal which parts need reinforcement before the next upgrade. Just like debugging a program, these moments reveal what still needs to be healed and updated. You weren't made wrong. You were made to evolve.

The more you understand your settings, the more empowered you become. You stop fighting your avatar's story and start working with it. You decode your patterns. **You reclaim your power.** And you realize that everything was preparing you to remember who you are.

Because once you know the game features, you can finally start to **play on purpose**. Not perfectly. Not without challenge. But with clarity, choice, and power.

Reflection Prompt

- What have you judged about your upbringing that might actually be part of your soul's mission?
- In what ways did your early environment or birth circumstances help shape the lessons your soul came here to learn?
- What "difficulty level" do you think you're playing on — and what has it taught you?
- What side quests have brought you the most joy?

Next Level: Simulation Code – How Beliefs Shape Your Reality

Now that you've explored the game's external features — your avatar, your karmic level, your mission, and your chosen setup — it's time to go internal.

Because behind every experience in your simulation... there's a belief running the code.

In Chapter 6, we'll uncover the hidden programs shaping what loads into your life: the subconscious beliefs, emotional frequencies, and inner scripts that determine how your reality responds.

This is where the real rewiring begins.

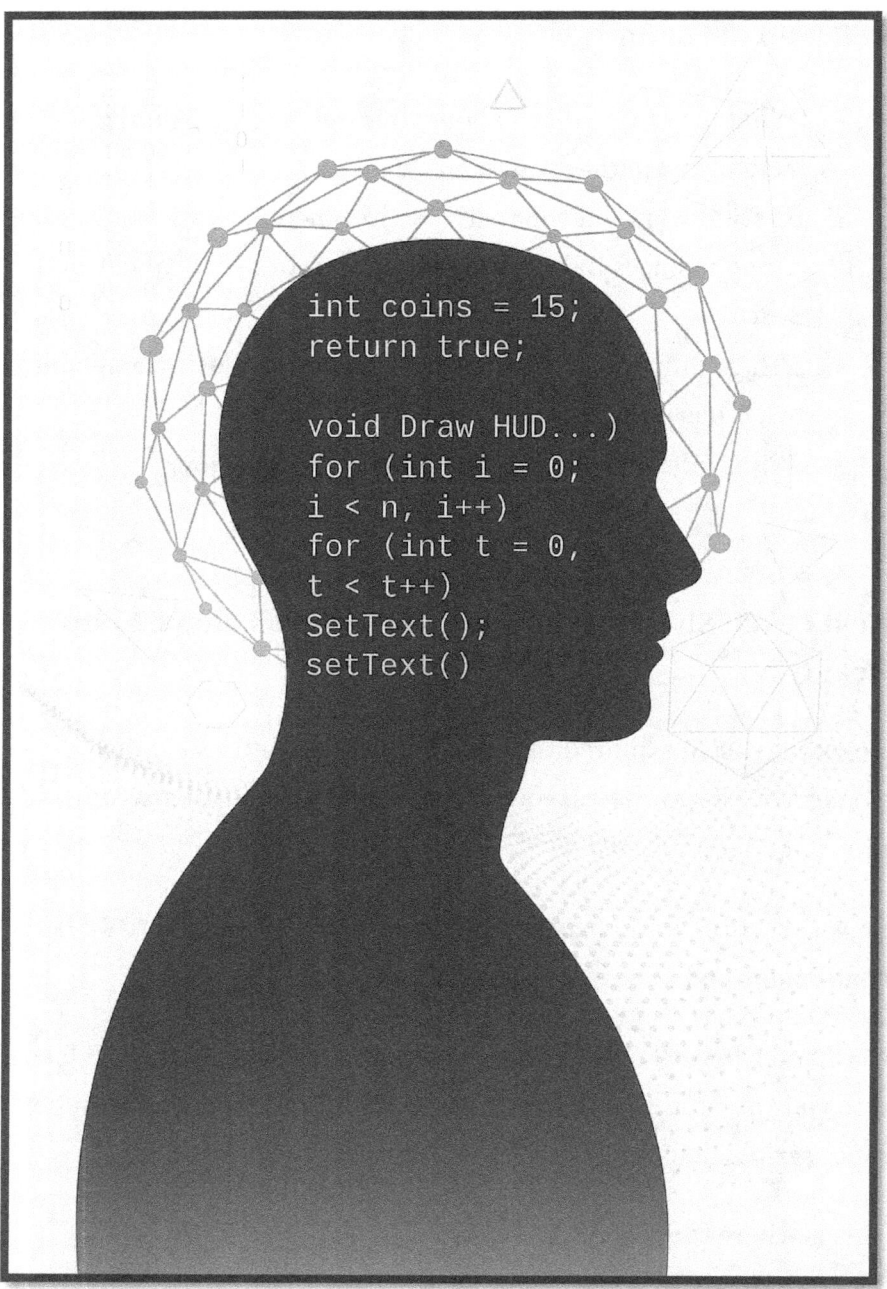

CHAPTER 6: SIMULATION CODE – HOW BELIEFS SHAPE YOUR REALITY

What if your beliefs weren't just ideas, but the actual code that determines how your simulation renders?

Your belief system isn't just personal — it's structural. It filters what you perceive, how you interpret, and what even shows up on your radar. In this chapter, we'll unpack how your beliefs create your version of the Game, how they're formed, how they're inherited, and how to update them when they're no longer aligned.

Beliefs Are the Code of the Simulation

Most people are still running on an outdated operating system — slow, reactive, and full of fear-coded commands. Healing isn't just about adding spiritual routines or better self-care apps. It's about upgrading your entire internal software — from survival mode to soul-level sovereignty.

When you rewrite your beliefs and emotional code, it's like upgrading from dial-up to high-speed VR. The system becomes user-friendly. The world becomes more alive. You don't just process reality — you engage with it on a higher frequency. Suddenly, life responds faster. Colors feel brighter. Opportunities appear where there used to be obstacles. And you have access to programs (possibilities) you didn't even know existed. Suddenly, life responds faster. Reality gets more colorful. You don't just see more — you feel more.

Beliefs function like the operating system of your avatar. They aren't just thoughts — they're embedded frequencies that silently dictate how your reality loads.

Your beliefs tell your brain and body how to respond, what to expect, and what to ignore. If you believe "people always let me down," your system will scan for and highlight every moment that supports that belief. You'll filter out anything that contradicts it — not because it's untrue, but because it doesn't match the code.

This isn't about being delusional — it's about understanding how the simulation responds to your **signal**. Your beliefs emit a dominant frequency, and that frequency acts like a tuning fork. It determines what kind of experiences you attract, what opportunities you recognize, and how you interpret them.

Beliefs are the language of the subconscious — and the subconscious runs the show. That means you're not seeing life as it is. You're seeing it as you were conditioned to believe it should be.

The simulation is a responsive field. Your belief system sets the parameters of what's possible inside it. Change your beliefs, and you change your version of reality — instantly, subtly, and profoundly.

Where Do Beliefs Come From?

Beliefs aren't just thoughts — they're the subconscious architecture of your avatar. Think of them as lines of invisible code quietly shaping what the simulation renders.

Your beliefs didn't materialize out of nowhere — they were shaped by everything you've seen, felt, absorbed, and survived. Most were installed long before you were aware they were optional. Understanding where they come from gives you the power to untangle what's truly yours.

Inherited beliefs from your family, culture, and environment: These are passed down like spiritual DNA. You might carry beliefs about money, love, success, or identity that originated generations before you. These can include survival-based thinking, limiting traditions, or subconscious roles inherited from your ancestry.

Imprinted beliefs from early experiences and trauma: The brain is most impressionable in childhood, especially from ages 0–7 when you're in a theta brainwave state — like a walking subconscious sponge. During this time, you download emotional blueprints from your caregivers, school, religion, and community. A single moment — being shamed, left out, or scolded — can install a belief that echoes for decades.

Collective beliefs from society, media, religion, and group identity: These are the ideas you absorb by participating in a shared reality. Cultural myths, media narratives, and religious conditioning can program entire populations to believe in lack, hierarchy, punishment, separation, or unworthiness. You can be plugged into belief systems without even realizing it — until you try to live outside them.

Chosen beliefs you've consciously accepted based on your own reflection or healing: These are the beliefs you create on purpose. The ones you install after introspection, education, inner work, or divine downloads. They may begin as borrowed ideas from mentors or books, but over time, they crystallize into your chosen truth.

Most of your core beliefs were formed between ages 0–7, while you were absorbing life in theta state. You didn't choose them — they were uploaded like a software package. Some protect you. Some limit you. Some conflict with your truth. But all of them are modifiable.

Belief Levels – A Map of Expansion

Beliefs tend to evolve in layers, like levels in a video game. Each level unlocks new perception, new potential, and a different version of reality. What once felt impossible becomes normal. What once felt threatening becomes safe. This is how growth reveals itself — not through leaps, but through subtler shifts in what you believe to be true.

Area of Life	Limiting Beliefs	Expansive Beliefs
Self Worth	"I'm not good enough"	"I am sacred and whole without needing to prove anything"
	"I'm doing my best"	"I have value regardless of output"
Money	"Money is evil"	"Money is just energy — I am the source"
	"Money is a tool"	"Money flows to me when I'm in alignment"
Relationships	"Love is painful"	"Love is who I am"
	"Love is conditional"	"Love is growth"
Spirituality	"God is watching and judging"	"I am a living expression of Source"
	"God is loving but separate from me"	"God lives within me"

Each new level of belief doesn't just change your mindset — it changes your frequency. It changes what the simulation mirrors back to you.

That's why healing and mindset work can feel like reality itself is shifting — because it is.

Even a small but sincere shift in belief can collapse entire timelines and unlock paths that were invisible at the previous level. These jumps may feel sudden, but they're built on every previous belief you were willing to question.

This is how we evolve upward — one new belief, one new possibility, one new frequency at a time.

Real-Time Reprogramming – A Daily Alignment Reset

This is where the Player reclaims control from the avatar — where conscious awareness interrupts unconscious programming. It's the moment you stop running old scripts on autopilot and start rewriting your inner code with intention.

Think of it like debugging your internal software. Beliefs form passively through repetition and emotion — but changing them requires conscious presence, emotional honesty, and deliberate action.

This practice is your fast-acting belief reset — a simplified reprogramming technique you can use in real time to interrupt old patterns, shift your state, and reconnect with your empowered frequency.

It simplifies the full process taught in Chapter 13: Boss Level – Recoding the Simulation from the Inside Out, but in a condensed format for everyday use. When you notice yourself feeling triggered — emotionally activated, reactive, or stuck in a familiar pattern — this is the tool you reach for.

Think of it as your daily mental tune-up. A small shift here can ripple into big results everywhere.

Quick Steps for In-the-Moment Shifts

Identify → Challenge → Rewire

Step 1: Identify the Belief

✦ Ask yourself: *What thought is shaping my experience right now?* What emotion is it producing? Is this belief something I consciously chose — or something I absorbed?
Does it reflect who I truly am and where I'm going, or is it an old loop replaying by default?

Step 2: Challenge the Belief

✦ Ask yourself: *Is this belief absolutely true?* Who taught me this, and does it still serve who I'm becoming?
Tune into your body — does this belief feel empowering or limiting?
If it brings contraction, shame, or fear, it may be a false program running beneath the surface.

Step 3: Rewire the Belief

Speak or write a new belief that reflects your truth.
Visualize yourself living from this new belief — how would you think, feel, act, and respond if it were already true?
Anchor the new frequency into your body through breath, movement, or emotion. The more you embody it, the more your system begins to adopt it as your new normal.

Take one small aligned action, even symbolic, that reinforces your new belief in the real world. This proves to your subconscious that the change is safe — and happening now.

Belief reprogramming is less about flipping a switch and more about layering in new truths until they feel just as familiar as the old ones once did. Your subconscious learns by repetition and emotion.

Neuroscience confirms that the brain is plastic — it changes in response to focused thought and emotional experience. This is why pairing affirmation with visualization and aligned action creates stronger neural rewiring than words alone. So the more often — and more fully — you practice the new belief, the more naturally it becomes your new baseline. Research shows that combining mental rehearsal with physical movement creates deeper neural encoding — meaning the belief becomes embodied, not just conceptual.

When you change your belief, you shift your frequency. When you shift your frequency, the version of the Game that loads around you changes too.

Ready to Go Deeper?

This quick reset is powerful — but sometimes, a belief feels too sticky or the shift doesn't hold. That's not a failure — it just means it's time to go deeper.

*Turn to **Chapter 13: The Reprogramming Protocol – A New Blueprint for Transformation** when you're ready to trace the root of a belief, unravel emotional entanglements, and fully rewire your subconscious blueprint.*

Beliefs Aren't Truths — They're Filters

Just because you believe something doesn't mean it's true. It simply means it's active in your subconscious — and that activation is shaping your perception.

Beliefs act like frequency-specific lenses. They tint how you interpret people, events, opportunities, and even your own value. That's why two people can experience the exact same situation and walk away with radically different conclusions — because they're filtering the moment through different internal programming.

The brain is a pattern-recognition machine. It looks for evidence to confirm what you already believe and ignores what doesn't fit. This is called **confirmation bias**. It's your brain's way of creating consistency between your inner world and your outer experience — even if the belief is harmful. The simulation matches what the system believes is real — and it keeps your reality stable, even if it's painful. That's why changing a belief can feel disorienting at first. It doesn't just shift your thoughts. It shifts your entire worldview.

When you start seeing beliefs as filters — not absolute truths — you become free to try on new ones. You stop asking, "Is this true?" and start asking, "Is this useful? Is this aligned? Does this move me forward?"

This doesn't mean bypassing or pretending everything is great. It means choosing your perspective **on purpose** — not defaulting to old code just because it's familiar.

Because if you don't consciously choose your beliefs, you're still

89

being programmed — just by someone else.

In a responsive simulation, your belief isn't just a lens — it's a launcher. It activates the version of the Game that responds to who you're becoming. And every new belief you choose becomes a step into that upgraded reality.

Reflection Prompt

- What belief have you outgrown but still carry?
- Where do you think this belief originally came from?
- What new belief are you ready to install?

Next Level: Environmental Programming – How Your Space Shapes Your Frequency

You've rewritten the inner code — now it's time to update the outer field.

Because the simulation doesn't just respond to your beliefs — it reflects your surroundings. Your environment, relationships, and daily inputs all act like energetic amplifiers or limiters.

In Chapter 7, we'll explore how to curate your space, protect your energy, and align your external world to match your inner upgrades — so your evolution doesn't get overwritten by old noise.

CHAPTER 7: ENVIRONMENTAL PROGRAMMING – HOW YOUR SPACE SHAPES YOUR FREQUENCY

Your environment has a powerful impact on your frequency — and because your frequency determines which version of reality you align with, it plays a central role in how the simulation unfolds around you.

Every space you occupy — your home, your car, your workspace, even your digital feed — either reinforces your current vibration or nudges it up or down. This is why awareness of your surroundings is so important. Think of your personal frequency as a number. If you're vibrating at 100 and walk into a space vibrating at 25, you're likely to feel pulled down. Energetic fields seek equilibrium — so when your frequency enters a space, the system recalibrates. Either the room rises to meet you, or you unconsciously dim to blend in.

This chapter is about understanding how physical environments — without even involving people — can influence your emotions, thoughts, nervous system, and trajectory. We'll explore how certain spaces can regulate your nervous system and support expansion, while others can stagnate or dysregulate you. Stories of haunted houses and emotionally heavy rooms aren't just legends — they're energetic truths. Energy lingers. It echoes. It loops until it's cleared — or amplified. And it can absolutely influence your state.

You're in a constant energetic exchange with your environment — like Wi-Fi signals syncing between your field and the simulation. Every room, object, scent, and sound contributes to your internal state. So in this chapter, we'll focus on how to clean, align, and intentionally design your space to support the version of you that you're becoming.

Environmental Safety – How Your Nervous System Reads the Room

Before you worry about how aesthetically pleasing a space is — or even how "high vibe" it feels — ask yourself one simple question: *Do I feel safe here?*

Safety is the foundation for healing, growth, and frequency elevation. Your body and nervous system register safety far more accurately than your mind. You can fake gratitude or light incense all day, but if your system is locked in fight-or-flight, the space is not supportive. Your vagus nerve, which plays a key role in regulating your nervous system, is constantly scanning your surroundings for cues of safety or danger. This happens faster than thought — your body feels the truth before your mind can label it.

A safe space is one where your nervous system can settle, your breath can deepen, and your energy doesn't feel like it's bracing or contracting. When your nervous system is regulated, your avatar functions at its highest potential. You're able to receive intuitive downloads, observe instead of react, and act from the Player rather than survival code. Regulation isn't about being calm all the time — it's about having the capacity to stay connected to yourself even when things get loud. It's the fertile ground where alignment becomes possible.

Without safety, the simulation feels like a trap. With safety, it becomes a playground for transformation.

Environmental Memory — When the Space Holds the Story

Spaces hold stories — whether you hear them or not.

Have you ever walked into a room and immediately felt heavy, unsettled, or drained — even if everything looked perfectly normal? That's not just your imagination. Every space carries an energetic memory. Emotions, arguments, grief, stress, celebration — they all leave vibrational imprints, like fingerprints on the walls of the simulation.

If the space once held personal experiences — especially traumatic or emotionally intense ones — the frequency lingers even more deeply. A room where you had your worst panic attack, grieved a loss, or felt trapped in a toxic loop may hold that energetic weight until it's intentionally cleared — or you physically remove yourself. Your body remembers, and so does the room.

Some places carry the residue of unprocessed energy — what people call "bad vibes." It's why hospitals can feel dense, why cemeteries feel sad, and some houses make you feel uneasy. The frequency of what occurred there echoes in the environment and interacts with your system.

Your nervous system is always listening — even when your mind isn't.

This is why energetic hygiene matters. Because without it, you're living in someone else's emotional leftovers — or your own. And the longer you stay immersed in that static, the more it becomes part of your frequency baseline. You're not just living in the space — you're syncing with its story.

Environmental Hygiene – Clearing the Frequency of Your Space

Your physical space, like your body, holds energetic residue. Every conversation, emotion, and event leaves a subtle imprint — like fingerprints on a window. And just like grime builds up if you never clean the glass, your environment can accumulate static that clouds your clarity and lowers your frequency.

This is why some spaces feel heavy and chaotic, while others feel calm and expansive. It's not just the decor. It's the data in the field.

You don't need to be a sage-burning crystal collector to tune a space (although that's cool too). Simple practices — like opening windows, moving furniture, clearing clutter, playing music, or setting intentions — can completely shift the vibration of a room.

So ask yourself: Is this space raising my signal or draining it? Is the energy here expanding me or looping me?

Energetic hygiene isn't about control — it's about clarity. The more tuned your environment, the easier it is to hold your frequency and create intentionally. You can't change what you're not aware of. But once you start noticing how your outer space affects your inner space, you unlock a whole new layer of the Game.

Digital Environment — What You Scroll Programs Your Field

Your phone isn't just a tool — it's a tuning fork. Every scroll syncs your field with what you consume.

Just like your physical space, your digital environment is an energetic field. Every notification, post, comment, app, and browser tab leaves a residue. And because you're interacting with this space so frequently, it has a direct impact on your emotional state, nervous system, and frequency.

Think of your phone as a portal to parallel energy fields. Who and what you give attention to through it is who and what you are aligning with energetically.

You're not just absorbing information — you're exchanging energy.

So it's worth asking: Is your feed feeding your future, or reinforcing your fears? Are you curating inspiration or spiraling through distraction?

Just like your physical space needs intentional clearing, your digital space needs occasional energetic detox too.

Media Environment – How Stories Echo in Your System

Every story you consume runs like a background app in your subconscious — processing, looping, and imprinting long after the credits roll. Your digital space includes more than just social media. What you watch, binge, or play is programming you, too.

Movies, TV shows, and video games aren't just entertainment — they're immersive energetic environments. They impact your thoughts, mood, and subconscious through storylines, symbolism, music, and emotional activation.

That intense crime thriller or emotionally heavy series may be beautifully made — but if consumed repeatedly without awareness, it can reinforce fear, anxiety, or hopelessness. The same goes for video games filled with chaos, violence, or overstimulation. They're not "bad," but your nervous system doesn't always distinguish fiction from real emotional input.

The goal isn't censorship — it's consciousness. Use your entertainment like a tool:

- Choose shows that inspire your creativity, compassion, or imagination
- Take breaks from media that consistently leaves you drained or numb
- Notice how certain content makes you feel — and how long the echo lingers

Your frequency is sensitive. Let your entertainment match the reality you're creating, not the one you're trying to escape.

Sound Environment – How Music Programs Your Emotional Field

Sound is one of the most powerful carriers of frequency in your environment. Neuroscience shows that repetitive sound and lyrics can influence mood, behavior, and memory — activating emotional centers and reinforcing neural patterns. Music doesn't just set a vibe — it embeds energy into your field. A song's tempo, tone, and especially its lyrics can elevate your frequency, soothe your nervous system, or unintentionally loop you into low-vibration thought patterns.

When you're singing along with music, you're not just consuming — it's a form of subconscious programming. Repeating lyrics like mantras, especially ones about pain, scarcity, or chaos, can keep those frequencies active in your field without you even realizing it. That emotional frequency can then influence your actions, thoughts, and even what your simulation reflects back to you.

That doesn't mean you can never listen to emotional or intense music — it means becoming intentional about how often, when, and why. Just like you wouldn't eat junk food every day, the energy of your playlist deserves a conscious check-in.

Use music to your advantage:

- Play uplifting or calming music to shift the vibe of a room
- Use high-frequency soundtracks or healing frequencies to reset your system
- Be mindful of lyrics you sing or repeat — they shape your emotional baseline

You don't just listen to music — you *live in it.* So choose a soundtrack that moves you toward who you're becoming. Every environment you shape becomes an interface. Tune it like you mean it — your reality is listening.

Environmental Reset – Actions to Clear Stagnant Energy

Everything in your environment carries a frequency. Clothes from a painful chapter, objects from a past relationship, or even a dusty trinket you forgot was there — all of it broadcasts energy into your field.

Your space holds memory. And if you're not consciously curating it, you might be unintentionally tuning into outdated timelines.

Clearing space isn't just cleaning — it's recalibrating the simulation.

It creates energetic room for new thoughts, patterns, and possibilities to load in.

Here are some small, powerful resets:

- Let go of objects, clothing, or décor holding stagnant or painful energy
- Open a window while setting a fresh intention for your space
- Rearrange one item on your altar, shelf, or desk to invite movement
- Light a candle with the words "release and renew"

- Delete five apps or unfollow five accounts that drain your energy
- Change your phone wallpaper to reflect your current intention
- Turn off push notifications that hijack your peace
- Delete saved messages, images, or emails tied to old timelines

---

The more intentionally you interact with your space, the more powerful your frequency becomes. And that frequency doesn't stop with you — it radiates outward. It reprograms the field.

You become the anchor point in the room.

That's why so many spiritual traditions use **smoke, sound, water, and salt** to shift energy — they're just tools to signal: *"This space is being cleared."* But the strongest tool of all is your presence. A grounded, heart-centered human can transform a room just by being fully in it.

Reflection Prompt

- What space in your life feels most like your future self? What space feels most like your past?
- What's one small change you could make today to raise the frequency of your environment?

Next Level: Multiplayer Mode – How Relationships Reflect and Rewire Your Code

Your environment doesn't just reflect your frequency — it shapes it. But once other players enter the game? Everything gets amplified.

In Chapter 8, we step into **Multiplayer Mode** — where relationships become mirrors, catalysts, and coding partners. Whether it's a soulmate or a coworker, every interaction is part of your simulation's feedback system.

Relationships can activate triggers, awaken old programs, or accelerate your evolution. Some stretch you. Some soothe you. Some are here to wake you up. Because the people in your life aren't just part of the scenery — they're part of the code.

Let's decode how these connections reflect what you're ready to see — and how to stay in your frequency, even when others are running a different script.

CHAPTER 8: MULTIPLAYER MODE – HOW RELATIONSHIPS REFLECT AND REWIRE YOUR CODE

If your environment reflects your frequency, your relationships *amplify* it.

People aren't just characters in your simulation — they're mirrors, messengers, and catalysts for evolution. Every connection carries a frequency. Some lift you. Some trigger you. Some arrive just to activate the next version of you.

This chapter explores the frequency of human connection — how the people around you shape your field, reflect your programming, and challenge you to grow. Just as spaces have a vibration, so do souls. And your relationships, chosen or not, are a huge part of your path.

Frequency Sync — How Your Relationships Tune Your Signal

Your relational environment is just as powerful as your physical one — sometimes more. The people in your space aren't neutral. They're tuning forks. Whether conscious of it or not, you're constantly syncing, shielding, or reshaping based on the emotional frequencies around you.

Modern neuroscience shows we have **mirror neurons** — brain cells that mimic what we observe in others. That's why we unconsciously absorb moods, habits, and even limiting beliefs. It's not just emotional — it's biological. And it's energetic.

Surround yourself with people who uplift, stretch, and mirror your truth — and your simulation starts to feel more expansive. Think of a time when someone believed in you more than you believed in yourself — and how that shifted your sense of what was possible. That's frequency transfer in action.

But stay entangled with those who drain, manipulate, or stay stuck in old loops — and you'll feel like you're stuck there too.

Whether empowering or draining, every relationship is an opportunity to observe the code you're syncing with — and choose whether to update it.

Because the more consciously you engage with your relational field, the more clearly you see what's yours to heal, what's ready to evolve, and what's no longer aligned with your Player's path.

When you develop healthy energetic boundaries, you stop absorbing other people's energy as your own — and start stabilizing your signal instead of shape-shifting to stay safe. Boundaries act as filters — not walls — helping you stay rooted in your own frequency rather than constantly shifting to match others. This steadiness not only protects your energy, it amplifies it.

According to **Polyvagal Theory**, your nervous system constantly scans for cues of safety or threat in others. When you maintain energetic boundaries, you send your system a message: "I'm safe in myself."

Think of energetic boundaries like the **force fields in a video game** — they don't block connection, but they stabilize your character so you can choose your response rather than absorb every incoming signal.

As you continue raising your vibration — clearing patterns, healing old versions of yourself, and anchoring into your core frequency — your reality will naturally shift. People who no longer match your frequency may fade away, while others who align more closely will begin to appear. And sometimes, even the people already in your life begin to show up differently — reflecting the shift in your frequency. This isn't rejection — it's resonance.

There's a reason people say, "Surround yourself with the kind of people you want to become." It's not just motivation — it's frequency science. Every interaction is an exchange — and what you feel in someone else is often a reflection of what's alive (or unhealed) in you. Now that you understand how energy moves between people, it's time to go deeper — into the emotional mirrors, subconscious patterns, and activation points that live within your most triggering relationships.

Pre-Programmed Connections – Soul Contracts & Karmic Loops

Some relationships feel magnetic, intense, or instantly familiar — not because of coincidence, but because of alignment. These are often what we call soul contracts: energetic agreements made before incarnation to help us evolve, remember, and resolve unfinished business.

Think of soul contracts like game missions you agreed to before hitting start — some are collaborations, some are challenges, but all are designed to help you level up.

Soul contracts aren't always gentle. Some come through pain, loss, or conflict. They're designed to stretch your soul's capacity, activate healing, and awaken awareness. That person you "can't shake" or keep crossing paths with? They may be helping you close a karmic loop.

A karmic loop might look like dating different people who abandon you — different names, same outcome. It's not a punishment — it's a pattern asking to be healed. The moment you identify the root wound (*I'm not worthy of consistent love,* for example) and truly shift it, the loop dissolves. The pattern no longer serves a purpose.

Some of these loops aren't even yours — they may be inherited from your lineage. Studies in epigenetics show that trauma can pass through generations, until someone breaks the cycle.

Soul contracts also have a natural life span. Once the lesson is integrated, the contract may be complete. You might feel an emotional release, notice the trigger is gone, or realize the relationship is naturally fading. Not all soul connections are meant to last forever — some are just meant to change you.

Divine timing plays a role too. Certain people enter your life exactly when your frequency aligns with theirs — or when a pivotal lesson is ready to unfold. Sometimes, raising your frequency is what unlocks the timing of a long-delayed connection. The people you're meant to meet can't find you until you're vibrating on the same level.

Trusting the timing doesn't mean forcing the connection. It means honoring the sacred intersection without clinging to the form it takes.

In this simulation, relationships aren't random. They're data, design, and divine choreography. Your soul knows who to meet, when to meet them, and what it came to learn.

Emotional Echoes – Relationship Triggers as Reflection Points

What if the people who drive you the most crazy are actually the ones showing you what's still unhealed?

That's not just a nice reframe — it's the mechanics of how the simulation works. Your external world reflects your internal programming, and nothing reflects it faster than your relationships. Conflict, irritation, people-pleasing, abandonment fears — they're all projections of the code you came here to update.

In Jungian psychology, this is called shadow work — learning to recognize and integrate the disowned parts of yourself that others reflect back to you.

The next time you feel triggered, ask: *What part of me is being activated here? What belief is this situation trying to make visible?* It might be a wound. It might be a story you're ready to rewrite. Either way, the person in front of you is just the mirror — not the source.

This doesn't mean you should tolerate mistreatment — it means you can use the reaction as data, while still honoring your boundaries.

And the beauty of mirrors? You don't need to smash them. You just need to adjust what's being reflected.

You do this by identifying the version of you that's being mirrored — then giving that part compassion instead of judgment. Is it your abandoned inner child? Your people-pleasing protector? Your wounded teen self that learned to push love away? When you spot it, pause. Breathe. Offer love to the version of you that's still seeking healing.

For example, if someone makes you feel invisible or rejected, instead of spiraling into blame or shame, you might realize: *This is reflecting a younger version of me who felt unseen in childhood.* Then you can say to yourself: *"I see you now. I love you. You don't have to fight for visibility anymore."*

In a simulation, mirrors aren't flaws in the system — they're feedback mechanisms. They show you which part of your code is still active.

This doesn't mean the external situation is ideal — but it means you've reclaimed your power to shift it from within.

And when you heal that part in you, you'll stop attracting or being affected by that pattern in the same way. It won't stick to your frequency anymore. It becomes neutral — because it's no longer active.

This healing process can be accelerated using the tools we've covered in other chapters: journaling, self-dialogue, subconscious reprogramming, and especially Quantum Reprogramming™ — where you go deep into the root and rewire the belief, not just the behavior. Quantum Reprogramming™ is the process of shifting your inner frequency through subconscious, emotional, and energetic alignment — so you stop repeating the same outcomes with different faces.

When you consistently meet that part of yourself with love and retrain your autopilot, the mirror finally reflects a new version of you.

Co-Regulation Codes – Rewiring Through Safety & Support

In fact, safe relationships do more than just feel good — they can **rewire your nervous system**. Neuroscience shows that our nervous systems are wired for connection. The **vagus nerve**, a key stress regulator, responds to the tone of someone's voice, their body language, and even their emotional state. Safe people help calm our system — without us even realizing it.

Safe doesn't mean perfect. It means consistent, kind, and emotionally present. People whose energy says, "You don't have to perform here."

Through co-regulation, your body learns a new baseline of safety, softness, and steadiness. Over time, being around someone who is emotionally grounded can help retrain your own responses to stress, connection, and vulnerability.

These environments also support the reprogramming of old beliefs. When you are consistently met with kindness, respect, and compassion, the subconscious begins to accept a new truth: *I am worthy of this.* That kind of repeated exposure becomes healing in itself.

Safe people increase your capacity for self-love — not just through support, but by giving you a mirror of who you are when you're no longer surviving. They mirror back the version of you that exists when you're regulated, not surviving — when your essence can lead instead of your defenses.

Let's define what we're really building here:

- **Self-love** is the ability to accept, nurture, and care for yourself emotionally, physically, and spiritually.
- **Confidence** is the trust in your ability to take aligned action, speak your truth, and navigate challenges.
- **Self-esteem** is your felt sense of worthiness — how much you value yourself and believe in your right to belong, succeed, and be loved.

Safe relationships support all three — and they show you what becomes possible when love isn't conditional or chaotic.

Reflection Prompt

- Who in your life feels emotionally safe, calming, or regulating to be around?
- What relationship pattern are you currently being shown — and what might it be trying to teach you?
- Where are you still trying to be understood instead of simply staying aligned with your frequency?
- Who reflects the most authentic version of you — and who mirrors an outdated self you're ready to release?

Next Level: Collective Mode

You've seen how your energy shapes your environment — and how relationships act like multiplayer mirrors that reflect, trigger, and upgrade your code. But this simulation isn't single-player.

Welcome to **Collective Mode** — where your frequency plugs into the global server of humanity. Every shift you make uploads to the field. Every breakthrough adds data. Your healing isn't just personal — it's planetary.

In the next chapter, we'll explore how shared energy shapes reality on a massive scale — how fear spreads, how hope multiplies, and how we co-create the next level of the Game together.

CHAPTER 9: COLLECTIVE MODE – HOW SHARED ENERGY CODES OUR REALITY

If your frequency creates your experience, imagine what happens when billions of frequencies interact.

This is the collective field — an energetic ecosystem made up of every thought, belief, wound, hope, fear, and breakthrough on the planet. We're not just individuals running isolated simulations. We're co-creators in a networked simulation, constantly influencing and being influenced by each other's energy.

Some parts of the collective are heavy with old programming — generational trauma, fear-based systems, societal conditioning. Other parts are rising — communities focused on healing, consciousness, and embodied love. The balance between these determines the "weather" of the simulation: what's trending, what's shifting, what's ready to collapse, and what's being born.

The more fragmented the collective becomes, the more powerful a coherent frequency becomes. Your clarity is part of the cure.

This chapter explores how your personal healing affects the collective — and how tuning into the collective can clarify your personal mission.

Think of the collective field like a shared group chat. Every thought, feeling, or outburst you send into it shapes the vibe — and everyone else can feel the ripple, whether they know it or not.

Multiplayer Impact – How Your Inner Work Updates the Field

Just like your thoughts shape your world, the collective thoughts of humanity shape the world we all live in. Every time you heal a pattern, embody your truth, or raise your frequency — you don't just change your own reality. You send out ripples.

You've probably felt this. The way a calm person can ground a chaotic room. The way fear spreads faster than facts. The way one voice of authenticity can inspire dozens to speak up.

That's the collective field in motion.

Every emotion you transmute, every belief you rewrite, and every old pattern you release adds a new vibration to the shared field. It's like uploading upgraded code that others can then access — sometimes without even realizing it.

So while your personal journey is yours alone, it's also contributing to something bigger. You're a node in the network. A fractal of the whole. When you do your inner work, it's not selfish — it's sacred service.

> *This ripple effect has even been observed in nature. In a famous study, scientists observed a group of monkeys on a remote island who began washing their sweet potatoes before eating them. Over time, more monkeys on that island adopted the behavior. But then something surprising happened — monkeys on entirely separate islands, who had no physical contact with the original group, began washing their food too. The behavior spread through the collective consciousness.*
>
> *Just like those monkeys, your energetic upgrades have the power to influence the Field far beyond your direct reach.*

In game terms, every personal upgrade sends a patch to the shared system — it updates the code for all players with access to that vibration.

Your healing becomes a frequency beacon that others can tune into. You help normalize new timelines just by walking them first.

BE THE VERSION YOU WANT TO SEE!!!

Simulation Surges — How Global Events Spark System Shifts

The collective field isn't just shaped by our personal healing — it's also influenced by planetary and cosmic rhythms.

Take the **Schumann Resonance**, for example — the electromagnetic frequency of Earth's atmosphere. Spikes in this frequency have been linked by some researchers and spiritual teachers to increased awakening symptoms, emotional upheavals, and expanded states of consciousness.

Solar flares can have similar effects. These bursts of solar radiation affect Earth's magnetic field and, according to some theories, also impact our own energetic systems — especially our emotional regulation and nervous system balance. Just like an energetic surge in your own body can trigger a release, solar activity may spark mass emotional purging or epiphanies — like a system-wide update hitting everyone's dashboard at once.

And then there's **astrology**. Planetary transits, retrogrades, eclipses, and collective nodal shifts often mirror the energy themes humanity is moving through. These aren't just personal — they're collective software updates, influencing what rises to the surface, what heals, and what breaks open.

We've seen this play out in recent history. The **COVID-19 pandemic** wasn't just a global health crisis — it was a collective energetic event. It activated fear, uncertainty, grief, and reevaluation on a planetary scale. It revealed fractures in systems and relationships. But it also created space for mass awakening, slowed time, and sparked questions like: *What really matters? What do I want to return to? Who am I when everything stops?*

These aren't just events — they're energetic invitations for recalibration.

Other moments — like the rise of social justice movements, global protests, or sudden shifts in technology — also represent **frequency shocks to the simulation**. They amplify unresolved energy while opening portals for change.

Whether you see these phenomena as symbolic or literal energetic influencers, they offer one clear message: we are not separate from the cosmos. We are deeply wired into the greater field of consciousness.

Collective triggers (like world events, social media firestorms, or viral trends) often activate unresolved energy in the masses. It's not just about what's happening — it's about what it stirs up in the human psyche. This is why shadow work and integration are so important. Because the more grounded and clear you are, the less you get pulled into the collective swirl — and the more you can anchor light in the middle of it.

Shadow work is the inner-game strategy that keeps you from being pulled into glitch loops created by unresolved collective pain.

Soul Server – How the Akashic Field Stores Simulation Data

Psychologist Carl Jung called this shared energetic space the **collective unconscious** — a reservoir of symbols, instincts, and patterns that live beyond individual awareness. What mystics call the **Akashic Field**, Jung might've described as **archetypal memory**. Both suggest that we're wired into something much larger than ourselves.

The Akashic Field is often described as a vast energetic record of every thought, emotion, intention, and soul journey across time and space. You can think of it as the **soul server of the simulation** — a spiritual iCloud where every frequency gets backed up and made available to the field.

Every decision you make, every belief you hold, every lesson you integrate — it all leaves an imprint. When you shift your vibration, you're not just changing your own level of play. You're uploading a new signal that others can subconsciously access, draw from, or resonate with.

Whether accessed through dreams, meditation, intuition, or deep energetic work, the Akashic Field is often viewed as a source of both guidance and pattern recognition. It doesn't just store what was — it reflects what's possible.

In game terms, every time you **upgrade your code** — by healing, remembering, or realigning — you make that version available in the collective archive. Your progress becomes a path that others can energetically follow.

Healing is personal. But remembrance is collective.

Frequency Anchors — Stabilizing the Simulation from Within

In chaos theory, this is known as the **butterfly effect** — where the smallest shift in one system can cascade into massive change elsewhere. The same applies here: when you shift your energy, you shift the simulation.

You didn't just come here to upgrade your personal experience — you came to anchor a new one into the collective field.

Change doesn't start with mass movements. It starts with one stable signal.

When you stay rooted in your truth, embody compassion, and live in alignment with your authentic frequency, you become a **stabilizing node in the network**. Your energy communicates what's possible without needing to say a word. You model an upgraded frequency just by being it.

You don't need to convince anyone. You just need to hold the signal.

Because **resonance rewires more than rhetoric ever could.**

And your field is always broadcasting.

Each time you hold your alignment during chaos, you act like a grounding circuit in the system. You prevent collective overload. You create coherence. And you invite others into regulation through your vibration.

When you hold your frequency with clarity and integrity, you don't just shift your life — you recalibrate the field itself. This is how simulations evolve: one anchored signal at a time.

You're not just a player. You're an anchor point. A transmitter. A walking patch note to the collective code.

Quick Reset Practice: Place your hand on your heart. Breathe deeply. Imagine your heartbeat sending light into the collective field. Ask: *What energy do I want to contribute today?*

Reflection Prompt

- What collective patterns do you feel most sensitive to — and what might that reveal about your soul's mission?
- How do you tend to react during collective upheaval or emotional waves?
- What kind of energy do you want to amplify in your communities — online and offline?
- How can you stay grounded in your truth without disconnecting from the world?

Next Level: Multiverse Access – Navigating the Multi-Frequency Simulation

So far, you've explored how your personal energy interacts with the world around you — your space, your relationships, and even the collective field. But what if every version of reality you've ever imagined is already real?

What if you're not just shaping reality — you're selecting it?

In the next chapter, we'll dive into the Multi-Frequency Simulation Theory — the core framework behind this entire book. You'll learn how each belief, emotion, and identity shift doesn't just influence your path — it literally changes the version of the simulation you're tuned into.

This is where you begin to access the multiverse.

You'll meet your parallel selves, explore the mechanics of timeline jumping, and discover how to consciously select the reality that matches your highest frequency.

Because you're not stuck in one life.

You're surfing infinite versions of it — every moment, every thought, every shift.

CHAPTER 10: MULTIVERSE ACCESS – NAVIGATING THE MULTI-FREQUENCY SIMULATION

If your frequency determines what version of the world you experience — what happens when you shift your frequency? Now, we zoom in on your personal interface — where moment-to-moment shifts in frequency don't just shape experience, they select the version of the Game you're playing. Do you simply change your mood... or do you change your entire reality?

Welcome to the **multi-frequency simulation theory**. It proposes that you are not living in a single version of reality but surfing across infinite vibrational layers — each one uniquely designed to match your internal frequency. Each layer, or "frequency field," is a version of reality rendered in real-time based on your inner state — like switching levels in a game with every new input.

You are the Player, shifting through versions of yourself and the world in every moment, even if the changes seem small. The multiverse isn't "out there" — you're living it now.

Frequency Coding — How Beliefs Tune You Into Your Reality

Back in Chapter 6, you explored how beliefs act as filters — shaping what parts of the simulation you're able to perceive. Now, we go deeper.

Beliefs aren't just filters. They're **frequency coding instructions**. They set the parameters for which version of the simulation loads around you. This lays the foundation for what we'll later explore as level jumping — each belief upgrade subtly or dramatically moves you to a different version of the simulation.

Every core belief you hold becomes a line of code in your energetic operating system. For example: a belief like "I have to work hard to be worthy" might render a simulation full of exhaustion, burnout, or conditional love — because the code demands it. If you believe life is hard, the simulation loads the version of reality that proves you right. If you believe you're supported, worthy, or lucky, the Game renders those truths back to you.

Think of your belief system like the source code behind a video game. The graphics, music, and storylines may change, but everything you see is generated by the code beneath. Shift the code, and the whole game changes.

That's why belief reprogramming is so powerful — and why we don't just do it mentally. It's not about repeating affirmations you don't believe. It's about shifting the **emotional signature** and subconscious pattern that your frequency is broadcasting.

Because in a frequency-based simulation, your beliefs don't just shape your thoughts — they tune you into the version of reality that matches their vibration. The simulation responds not to what you want, but to what your beliefs say is true. Shift the belief — and you shift the broadcast. It's not just theory — it's the energetic reason why small mindset changes often lead to massive shifts in how reality responds. The Game reacts to the code you're running — your subconscious beliefs, not just your desires.

Put simply? Your beliefs act like frequency settings. When you update those settings, you don't just feel different — you begin tuning into a different layer of the simulation entirely.

Level Jumping – How Beliefs Move You Across Realities

You don't force a new reality — you tune into it. Science shows your brain doesn't distinguish vividly imagined realities from actual events. In the quantum field, attention collapses potential into form — just like tuning an instrument determines the key the music plays in.

In a multi-frequency simulation, **level jumping** — what many people refer to as *timeline jumping* — isn't science fiction. It's the natural result of shifting your internal state. Every version of your life already exists in the field as a potential. What you experience is dictated by your alignment with one of those versions.

Think of level jumping like switching radio stations. The songs are already playing — you just need to tune into the frequency that broadcasts the one you want to hear. Likewise, your future doesn't need to be built — it needs to be selected.

Shifts in level can be subtle or dramatic. Sometimes they feel like new opportunities or people "randomly" entering your life. Other times, they show up as shifts in perception — where what once triggered you no longer hooks you — because you're not tuned to that version of yourself anymore. The more intentional your alignment, the more consciously you navigate to elevated levels.

Your **frequency** is the input that tells the simulation which version to load. It's what re-renders the pixels of your world in real time. When you align with a version of yourself who already lives the life you desire, the simulation shifts to reflect that. You don't bend reality — you shift to the version of reality that already matches your internal state.

Ask yourself:

- What version of me already lives the life I want?
- What beliefs, emotions, and behaviors does that version embody?
- What parts of me are still looping in an old frequency band?

You jump levels in the simulation by shifting your internal code — your thoughts, feelings, beliefs, and behaviors:

- Thinking differently
- Feeling differently
- Believing differently
- Acting differently

Every time you act in alignment with the higher version of you, you collapse into that level. It's not about "changing" the world — it's about changing your frequency so that the world you see changes around you.

And when you jump levels enough, you won't just feel different. Your whole life will look different, too. Your level is not a destination. It's a frequency. And you're holding the remote. Choose your channel with intention. The Game responds to your signal.

Avatar Variants – Accessing Your Alternate Selves

Every choice you've made — and didn't make — branches into a vibrational thread. Each thread is a version of you, alive and running within this quantum simulation. There's a version of you who pursued your dream. One who stayed small. One who spoke up. One who stayed silent.

These aren't just possibilities — they're active frequency streams, already encoded in the system. In quantum terms, this aligns with the Many-Worlds Interpretation: every choice collapses one potential, while others continue running in parallel.

The version you're currently experiencing isn't the "real" one — it's simply the one you're tuned into. You shift frequencies every time you change your thoughts, your state, or your sense of identity.

Think of it like loading a saved avatar in a game. Each one has its own stats, location, and gear. But they all live on the same cartridge. You don't create a new character — you just choose which one to play as based on the frequency you're embodying. It's not about becoming something new — it's about shifting your broadcast so that the simulation loads a version already stored in your energetic field.

You are not a single, static identity. You are a multiverse of selves, broadcasting through the lens of your current frequency. Your "main character" isn't fixed — it's fluid, selected moment to moment by how you think, feel, and behave.

Some versions of you are still stuck in loops, waiting for integration. Others are already living the level you're trying to reach. Some are born of trauma and fear. Others are encoded with your highest potential.

You don't unlock these versions — you embody them. Their data is stored in the field, waiting for resonance. The act of embodying is how you shift into their stream — but embodying that version requires more than insight. You align with it by tuning into the beliefs, emotions, and actions it runs on. What would that version of you believe? How would they feel? And what would they do differently right now?

The more aligned you are with your true self, the more liberating the level you enter. But when you're entangled in old programming, you default to versions shaped by fear, not freedom.

Level Drift and the Mandela Effect

Some people remember Nelson Mandela dying in prison. Others remember him becoming president. Some swear the Monopoly man had a monocle. Others say he never did. The Mandela Effect isn't just a quirky internet mystery — it's evidence of shifting levels.

As you change your frequency, you may access a version of reality that differs from the one you remember. Sometimes the changes are subtle. Other times, they're blatant. This is what happens when your consciousness moves faster than the collective field can update.

Memory glitches? Maybe. But if reality is rendered in real time, based on what you're aligned with — then these moments are proof you're no longer in the version of the game you used to be in.

When the world doesn't match your memory, don't assume you're wrong.

Assume you've leveled up.

Soul Signal – Connecting with Your Higher Self and Receiving Guidance

While "Avatar Variants" explored the different versions of you across frequencies, this section zooms out to introduce your Higher Self — the part of you that sees them all, guides you between them, and helps you align with your most expansive path.

Your Higher Self is the central intelligence in your soul's network — coordinating and observing every version of you across levels. It's the "player behind the avatar" — your eternal self that remembers who you are across all frequencies. That's why inner guidance often feels like wisdom from a future version of you — because it is. Think of your Higher Self as the main server, streaming insights and instructions to each avatar version based on your current level and readiness.

You can connect to parallel versions of yourself through dreams, meditation, or moments of deep reflection. These versions aren't fictional or imagined — they're real, energetic expressions of you that exist at different vibrational frequencies, playing out alternate choices, levels, and soul paths.

Each one represents a "saved state" in the simulation — versions of you that took a different route, healed a wound you're still holding, or stepped into a truth you've been afraid to claim. You don't imagine them — you resonate with them.

They show you what's possible. What's already healed. What you're capable of choosing next. They exist to help you course-correct, calibrate your frequency, and accelerate your growth by showing you what's already coded into your field — waiting to be tuned in.

Some versions of you hold keys. Others are caution signs. Your job isn't to collapse them — it's to listen, integrate, and align with the one that feels like your highest truth now.

You don't have to become all of them — you only need to align with the version of you that reflects your highest current truth. That's how you begin syncing your identity with your next-level self — and how your guidance system can finally lock onto your signal with clarity.

Your highest truth is often revealed through what sparks your joy, curiosity, and inner aliveness. Follow those breadcrumbs — they're not distractions, they're the coordinates.

Identity Sync — Broadcasting the Avatar You Align With

In a multi-frequency simulation, your identity isn't something you discover — it's something you broadcast. Your sense of self is not fixed — it's vibrational. It's determined by the frequency you consistently emit through your beliefs, emotions, habits, and choices.

You are not defined by your past. You are defined by the self you choose to embody right now.

This is your **vibrational identity** — the energetic signature that tells the simulation what kind of reality to render around you. It's less about what you think you are, and more about what version of you your frequency aligns with.

This is why personal growth can feel confusing or even scary. When you start healing old wounds and changing core beliefs, your frequency shifts — so the simulation starts loading a new version of your reality. People may fall away. New opportunities arise. Old environments feel misaligned. That's not regression — it's recalibration.

Each time you:

- Choose courage over fear,
- Rest when your old self would have hustled,
- Speak your truth instead of staying silent,
- Say no to what drains you,
- Or pursue what lights you up...

...you shift your vibrational identity. You send a new instruction to the field about who you are — and the simulation adjusts accordingly.

You don't become a new self — you align with a version of you that already exists at a higher frequency. Your job is to **stay in resonance** long enough for that new level to stabilize.

The more consistent your alignment, the more stable your frequency — and the more stable the new version of your reality becomes.

This is how you embody remembrance. Not by knowing who you are — but by living like it.

Support Team — Calling in Your Spirit Allies

You're not navigating this simulation alone.

Just like a co-op game gives you teammates to help you level up, you came into this lifetime with a **spirit support team** — a multidimensional squad working behind the scenes to guide, protect, and assist your soul's evolution.

Your **spirit allies** may include:

- **Your Higher Self** the part of you guiding from a broader, soul-level perspective
- **Guides** assigned to this lifetime
- **Ancestors** walking with you through blood or energy
- **Higher-dimensional beings** aligned with your frequency
- **Animal totems** or symbolic messengers from the field

These allies are energetically connected to your soul through resonance. In energetic terms, you are **entangled** — meaning your shift in frequency can initiate movement on their side too. And when you consciously reach out, the connection strengthens.

They will never override your free will — but when invited, they can amplify your clarity, smooth your path, and align you with support you didn't even know you needed.

You might feel them through:

- Sudden insights or strong intuitive pulls
- Repeating numbers, songs, animals, or synchronicities
- Dreams or vivid visuals during meditation
- Signs that keep showing up until you pause and listen

To deepen your connection:

- **Talk to them** like trusted teammates
- **Ask for guidance or confirmation**
- **Create space to receive** through stillness, nature, or ritual
- **Acknowledge the nudges** and give gratitude when things align

You're not just being watched — you're being supported. Every time you walk in alignment with your soul path, you send a ripple through your team's field too.

And they're not waiting for you to have it all together or be healed. They're with you now, reminding you:
You were never meant to do this alone.

Reflection Prompt

- What level are you currently tuned into — and how do you know?
- Who is a version of you you're ready to embody more fully?
- What thoughts, habits, or beliefs belong to a level you're ready to leave behind? And ready to move too?

Next Level: Remembrance Mode – Why the Soul Chose to Forget

You've explored how this simulation responds to your frequency, how beliefs code your experience, and how shifting your identity tunes you into new levels of the Game. You've remembered that you're not one self — but many — and that your Higher Self is guiding the entire journey.

So why would a soul choose to forget all of that?

In the next chapter, we'll step into **Remembrance Mode** — where the purpose of forgetting is revealed. You'll discover why amnesia is part of the soul's design, how every level was encoded with clues to wake you up, and why remembering who you are is the ultimate power move in the simulation.

Because the goal isn't perfection. It's remembrance.
And joy? That's the breadcrumb trail leading you home.

CHAPTER 11: REMEMBRANCE MODE — WHY THE SOUL CHOSE TO FORGET

Why would a soul made of Source choose to forget it is divine? Why would we create a game so painful, so complex, so full of contrast?

Because that's how we evolve.

The simulation was never punishment — it was permission. Permission to experience every facet of existence. Permission to play with darkness so we could discover the light. Permission to break and rebuild. To lose ourselves so fully that remembering who we are feels like a miracle.

Master Mode — Why Earth Is the Ultimate Soul Challenge

Earth isn't just a planet. It's a master-mode simulation designed for accelerated soul evolution. It combines full memory wipe, emotional intensity, free will, and rapid karmic cycling — all within a shared multiplayer format. The density is thick, the emotions are intense, and the contrast is sharp. It's the ultimate arena where free will and divine order intersect — where only those ready for Master Mode dare to play. It's where your soul gets to experience the most dramatic, dynamic, and transformative quests in existence.

This planet isn't a punishment — it's the proving ground of Master Mode.

Souls who choose Earth aren't new to the game. They're the ones brave enough to say yes to a world with heartbreak, confusion, injustice, and forgetting — and still believe in the possibility of love.

Earth offers what no other simulation can: the opportunity to feel deeply, to rise after falling, to love after loss, to create beauty out of chaos. It's the forge where courage is shaped and soul muscles are built. It's where timelines can collapse or expand with a single choice.

The game here is fast, even when it feels slow. Every relationship, every struggle, every moment of stillness or chaos is a portal for evolution.

We don't come to Earth for ease. We come for expansion.

Pain isn't the goal — but it's often the path. Through grief, loss, betrayal, and limitation, we get to feel the edges of separation so we can stretch into the truth of unity. This is where we earn our mastery — not for flawless performance, but for rising each time we fall. Not for remembering perfectly, but for remembering anyway. Not for perfection, but for perseverance. Not for never falling — but for always rising, remembering, and returning to love.

We come to crack open. To remember love through loss. To sculpt the soul with every scar.

Amnesia Mode – Remembering Through Forgetting

You can't remember if you never forgot.

The veil wasn't a glitch — it was the mist that made the stars invisible, so we could rediscover their light. It was not a mistake — it was an essential part of the Game. Forgetting our divine nature, our origins, and our multidimensionality allowed us to fully immerse in the simulation.

This was the soul's agreement before entering: *'Let me forget — so I can feel it all. Let me lose the map — so I can trust the compass inside.'* It let us experience the illusion of separation, the tension of duality, and the rawness of contrast.

If you came in knowing you were eternal, powerful, and infinitely connected to Source — you wouldn't feel the ache of longing, the heartbreak of perceived loss, or the thrill of rediscovery. You wouldn't wrestle with doubt, or earn faith through fire.

Forgetting stripped us of our map so that we could learn to navigate by intuition, by resonance, by truth that lives in the bones — not just in the intellect. The challenge of remembering while surrounded by noise and illusion is what makes the return so powerful.

When you remember who you are in a world that constantly tells you otherwise, you aren't just waking up — you're **activating soul-level mastery**.

You become the lighthouse for others. You become proof that the Game is winnable. And you reclaim the choice to love, to believe, and to rise — not because you were told to — but because your soul remembered how.

To walk through the darkness and still choose light...
To feel small and still act with love...
To forget who you are and still treat others as divine...
That's not just remembrance. That's how you win the Game.

Contrast Engine — How Darkness Activates Light

In a simulation of duality, everything is created through contrast. Light and dark. Comfort and pain. Connection and loss. You can't recognize truth without lies. You can't appreciate joy without knowing sorrow. And you can't truly choose love unless fear is also on the table.

This duality is not a flaw in the system — it's the foundation of learning. The shadows you face in life aren't barriers to your growth — they're the fuel for it.

Contrast shows you who you are by first showing you who you're not.

When things break down, when you're betrayed, when you're lost in grief — that's not failure. That's friction. And friction sharpens your edges, activates your compassion, and deepens your discernment.

Shadow work is the sacred practice of turning toward the parts of yourself you've hidden or disowned. It's not about fixing what's broken — it's about reclaiming what was forgotten.

Challenge isn't meant to defeat you — it's meant to stretch you. Think of it like resistance training for the soul. The heavier the challenge, the more power you build by rising through it.

Everything in your life that broke you open was also building you. The betrayals, the failures, the dark nights — they weren't glitches. They were guideposts.

The question isn't "Why did this happen to me?"
The better question is: "What did this awaken in me?"

Every challenge is a checkpoint. Every wound is an invitation. Every breakdown is a portal to a deeper remembrance.

Embodiment Code – How Being Fully You Rewrites Reality

Source wants to experience itself in **every** flavor. Every color, every tone, every contradiction and paradox. That includes you. Your exact vibration — your wounds, your wisdom, your quirks, your creativity, your heartbreak — it's all part of the cosmic design. You're not a glitch in the system. You're a necessary signal in the symphony of remembrance.

Your embodiment is part of the code. Every time you show up as your full self, you reprogram what's possible in this reality.

There has never been another soul with your exact frequency, perspective, and timeline. That makes your presence irreplaceable.

You didn't come here to copy and paste someone else's version of enlightenment. You came here to be **fully, fiercely, unforgettably you** — and in doing so, activate others by your example.

Authenticity is your transmitter. When you show up as your true self, you don't just align your life — you realign timelines. You send a ripple through the collective field that says, "It's safe to be real."

Your story matters — even the messy chapters. Your voice matters — even when it shakes. Your energy matters — even when you're in transition. Because when you embody your truth, you don't just remember — you help the rest of us remember too.

You're not an extra in someone else's story.
You're a main character in the cosmic play.

And your frequency is the key code that only you can broadcast.

Even your struggles add to your signal. The way you transmute pain, the way you rise after falling, the way you find humor in heartbreak — all of it tells the universe, "This version of Source is awake and alive."

You don't need to wait to be perfect to be powerful. You don't need to heal everything before you shine. You just need to be honest, present, and brave enough to keep broadcasting.

When your frequency is fully online, you don't just remember — you help others remember too.

Mission Complete — Love Was the Cheat Code All Along

Beneath every mission, every glitch, every heartbreak and breakthrough — there's one objective coded deeper than all the rest:

To remember love.
To become love.
To live love.

That's the cheat code hidden in plain sight — love was never the reward; it was the unlock.

Not just love that's easy. Love that's chosen. Love that includes your own reflection — even the parts you've hidden, shamed, or struggled to accept.

Love is the code that reactivates your highest timeline. It dissolves illusion, rewrites karma, and collapses separation. It's not a feeling — it's a frequency. A choice. A remembering.

You weren't sent here to escape your humanity.
You were sent here to infuse it with divinity.

To bring heaven into your home.
To bring Source into your cells.
To walk through grocery stores and grief, board meetings and breakups, and still carry the flame of remembrance in your chest.

Because love doesn't mean bypassing pain.
Love means meeting pain with presence.
Love means being the safe place for your own shadow.
Love means honoring your truth even when it's inconvenient.

You didn't come here to get it right.
You came here to remember it's all right.

And every step, every scar, every stutter and surrender is part of that sacred remembering.
Every moment you choose love — especially when it's hard — is a signal to the Field that says, "I remember who I am."

And every time you remember, you light the way for the rest of us, too.

Reflection Prompt

- What parts of your story once felt like punishment but now feel like preparation?
- Where have you already turned pain into power?
- What have you remembered about yourself that the world once made you forget?
- How can you honor your mission with more love, not more pressure?

Next Level: Embodiment Mode – Living the Remembrance Through Sacred Play

Remembering is the spark. But embodying what you remember — that's how you change the game.

In the next chapter, we'll explore how to make remembrance more than a moment of insight. You'll learn how to live it, move with it, and play with it — every day. Because the goal isn't just to wake up... It's to stay awake and create from that truth.

CHAPTER 12: EMBODIMENT MODE — LIVING THE REMEMBRANCE THROUGH SACRED PLAY

You didn't come here just to *remember* who you are. You came here to *embody* it — like uploading your soul's code into your daily operating system.

Knowing the truth is just the beginning. Embodying that truth — moment by moment, breath by breath — is the real mastery.

It's easy to feel aligned on a retreat or during a breakthrough. But can you hold that remembrance in traffic? While grieving? At the DMV?

True embodiment isn't measured by peak moments — it's revealed in the ordinary ones.

Can you choose stillness instead of snapping back? Set a boundary with grace? Speak truth without attachment?

That's embodiment. That's playing the Game *in* real life — not just learning the rules.

Integration Mode – When Wisdom Becomes Your Default

We live in a world that loves peak experiences — downloads, breakthroughs, epiphanies. But awakening isn't about stacking spiritual highs. It's about **integrating** the wisdom you receive into how you think, feel, relate, and choose.

Integration is harder than inspiration because inspiration moves the mind, but integration rewires the whole system.

A download without integration is just spiritual entertainment — insight without embodiment is noise in a pretty package. Real activation happens when that insight reshapes how you live.

Think of insight as a software update. Integration is what happens when that update installs across all your apps — your thoughts, your habits, your relationships.

It's easy to feel awakened in a meditation, on a retreat, or after a profound dream. But integration is what you do when you're triggered, tired, or in the middle of a mundane moment. It's how you respond when life presses the same old buttons — and you choose a new reaction.

Integration requires patience, compassion, and repetition. It's not about perfection — it's about presence. Can you show up with love, even when you're in pain? Can you embody your truth when no one is watching? Can you keep your frequency intact in the grocery store, not just the yoga mat?

Every integrated insight becomes part of your new default identity — the version of you that responds, relates, and radiates from remembrance, not reaction.

This is the sacred work. The quiet work. The part no one claps for — but the part your soul will thank you for the most. It's where the real game is played — and where your remembrance becomes a way of being, not just a flash of insight.

Integration doesn't shout. It stabilizes.

Your frequency is only as stable as your nervous system can hold.

That's why embodiment practices — like breathwork, somatic healing, conscious movement, creativity, nature connection, and nervous system regulation — are the bridge between insight and integration. They help you stabilize the shifts you've made so they become your new normal.

In moments of stress, ask: *What would my integrated self do here?* Then do that, even just 10% more.

Awakening isn't a moment.

It's a lifestyle.

You're not here to just visit higher frequencies — you're here to **become a stable broadcast of them.**

Checkpoints & Challenges – When Triggers Reveal the Code

Every challenge is a level marker. Every breakdown, heartbreak, rejection, or trigger is a **checkpoint** — not a punishment.

They don't mean you're off-path. They often mean you're right on it.

But instead of seeing them as walls, try viewing them as mirrors. This is where **shadow work** (facing the unconscious parts of yourself) and **mirroring** come in. Mirroring means the outer world reflects your inner patterns — especially the ones you're not fully conscious of yet. The things that irritate you, wound you, or repeat over and over are trying to show you what still needs your love, attention, or boundaries.

Once you realize the world is reflecting your inner patterns, the real power comes from asking the right questions:

- What is this challenge mirroring back to me?
- What emotion or pattern is being revealed?
- How can I offer compassion to the part of me that's still learning to feel safe?

Growth isn't about perfection. It's about *presence through discomfort*. And every time you stay present with a hard moment instead of numbing or fleeing — you level up.

Every trigger is an invitation to meet yourself with more truth, not more shame.

Examples of Checkpoints in Real Life:

- You're constantly overlooked at work → This may reflect an inner belief that your voice doesn't matter or fear of being seen.
- A romantic partner leaves without explanation → This could be mirroring abandonment wounds from childhood or a lesson in self-worth.
- A friend sets a boundary and you feel rejected → This might trigger an old pattern of people-pleasing and needing approval to feel safe.
- You feel envious of someone else's success → That emotion may be pointing you to your own buried desires and a limiting belief that you can't have it.

These aren't just random pains. They're precision-coded invitations to evolve. When you decode the trigger instead of reacting to it, you start rewriting the game from the inside out.

Even noticing the pattern is progress. Awareness is the first step to rewiring the code.

Emotional Compass — Navigating Truth with the Map of Consciousness

Living your truth doesn't mean always feeling good. It means being real — emotionally honest, energetically aligned, and unwilling to betray yourself for acceptance.

It's not about performing peace or chasing happiness. It's about being so rooted in your truth that you no longer need to please, prove, or pretend.

Emotional honesty keeps you in integrity with your authentic self — and that's one of the highest frequencies available.

Your authentic self is the version of you that exists beneath the programming. It's who you were before the world told you who to be. It's the part of you that vibrates with truth, love, and freedom — even if it got buried under years of shame, fear, or survival strategies.

Most of us have been trained to operate from a conditioned self — a version built from limiting beliefs, inherited trauma, and unconscious loops. This self isn't *bad* — it was built to keep you safe. But it's not your truth.

The more you release the layers of "should of" stories, and self-rejection, the closer you return to the signal of your authentic self. And that's when your vibration rises — not because you're fixing yourself, but because you're finally being yourself.

The **Map of Consciousness**, developed by Dr. David Hawkins, is a powerful tool that charts the vibrational frequency of emotional

156

states — from the dense weight of shame to the expansive energy of joy and peace. Shame and guilt sit at the bottom. Love, joy, and peace rise to the top.

Authenticity and enlightenment vibrate at the same frequency — because when you're fully aligned with your truth, you're no longer operating from fear or illusion. You're resonating as your highest self.

But this isn't about judgment — it's about awareness. The map isn't a ladder to climb — it's a mirror to see where you're standing, and a guide to help you return to truth.

You don't raise your frequency by <u>performing</u> happiness. You raise it by being **brave enough to feel what's real**.

Here's a simplified look at some of the emotional frequencies on the scale, listed from highest to lowest:

MAP OF CONSCIOUSNESS

	God-view	Life-view	Level	Scale	Emotion	Process	
P O W E R	Self	Is	Enlightenment	700-1000	Ineffable	Pure Consciousness	**S T R O N G**
	All-Being	Perfect	Peace	600	Bliss	Illumination	
	One	Complete	Joy	540	Serenity	Transfiguration	
	Loving	Benign	Love	500	Reverence	Revelation	
	Wise	Meaningful	Reason	400	Understanding	Abstraction	
	Merciful	Harmonious	Acceptance	350	Forgiveness	Transcendence	
	Inspiring	Hopeful	Willingness	310	Optimism	Intention	
	Enabling	Satisfactory	Neutrality	250	Trust	Release	
	Permitting	Feasible	Courage	200	Affirmation	Empowerment	
F O R C E	Indifferent	Demanding	Pride	175	Scorn	Inflation	**W E A K**
	Vengeful	Antagonistic	Anger	150	Hate	Aggression	
	Denying	Disappointing	Desire	125	Craving	Enslavement	
	Punitive	Frightening	Fear	100	Anxiety	Withdrawal	
	Disdainful	Tragic	Grief	75	Regret	Despondency	
	Condemning	Hopeless	Apathy	50	Despair	Abdication	
	Vindictive	Evil	Guilt	30	Blame	Destruction	
	Despising	Miserable	Shame	20	Humiliation	Elimination	

Anger, for example, vibrates **higher** than shame or guilt. That means allowing yourself to feel anger — rather than suppressing it — can actually move you up the scale. Emotional honesty, not forced positivity, is how you shift your vibration. You don't need to fake peace. You just need to keep honoring your truth.

Use the map like a compass, not a scoreboard. This isn't about judging where you are — it's about learning how to move with more awareness and less resistance. Think of it like a vibrational GPS:

- *What emotion is asking to be honored?*
  Name the truth without judgment.
- *Why am I feeling this?*
  Ask it more than once. Each layer reveals something deeper.
- *What belief is holding it in place?*
  Get curious about the story or fear beneath it.
- *What truth might emerge if I really feel this?*
  Let the emotion speak. Then let it go when it's ready.
- *What part of me needs love or reassurance right now?*
  This softens judgment and welcomes self-compassion.
- *If this emotion had a voice, what would it say?*
  Let your subconscious speak through the feeling.
- *What memory or experience is still echoing through this emotion?*
  This reveals stored energy waiting to be witnessed and released.
- *Is this feeling mine — or did I absorb it from someone else?*
  A powerful tool for empaths and sensitives to reclaim their frequency.

You don't leap from grief to joy. You soften into what's real — maybe grief wants to become anger. Maybe fear wants to become courage.

This is emotional alchemy. Not by fixing or forcing — but by witnessing. By staying close to what's real.

You can use this compass moment by moment:

- **Feeling anger?** *Ask yourself where it's coming from, and why. Let it rise fully, then listen — what is it protecting you from? What does it want you to know? When it's been honored, it may soften into courage or clarity.*
- **Sitting in guilt?** *Ask, "Who taught me this was wrong?" or "What part of me still believes I deserve punishment?" Trace it back, feel it through. The weight may lift as self-forgiveness begins to rise.*
- **Overwhelmed by fear?** *Let the fear speak. Ask it what it's trying to protect. When you hear its message, you may find space for neutrality, trust, or even empowerment.*

Use this compass whenever you feel off-center.
Even one honest check-in a day can shift your trajectory.

This isn't about climbing the scale — it's about clearing the charge. When you honor your real frequency, your system recalibrates. And over time, your baseline rises — authentically, not artificially.

Emotions = Energy in Motion

Emotions are energy in motion. When they're avoided or suppressed, that energy doesn't disappear — it stays stored in your system, anchoring your frequency at that vibrational level.

The goal isn't to bypass what you feel — it's to move through it. When you allow emotions to flow without judgment, you release the charge they carry. That's how you recalibrate back to your authentic frequency — clear, balanced, and aligned.

Don't shame your place on the map. Every conscious shift is an act of healing — and release.

> **Presence is the path.**
> **Awareness is the alchemy.**
> **Honesty is the elevation.**
> **Feeling is the release.**

That's how the map rewrites itself — from within.

Sacred Simulation – Finding the Divine in the Daily

When you stop chasing escape and start engaging with what's here, everything changes. The dishes become a mindfulness practice. Conversations become healing portals. Triggers become invitations. Even the glitches have meaning.

You are not in the way of your path. You're on it. And the "real world" isn't a distraction from your purpose — it's the exact level you came here to master.

Think of your life like a high-resolution, multidimensional quest designed with divine precision. Every moment — no matter how small or repetitive — is part of the simulation you coded to help you evolve. There are no filler scenes. There are no accidental characters. There are no wasted days.

Every interaction is a mirror. Every challenge is a checkpoint. Every seemingly boring day is an invitation to drop deeper into presence and mastery.

Living the remembrance means you stop waiting for enlightenment to arrive in some big, cinematic moment. Instead, you begin to see the sacred hiding in plain sight: in your breath, your body, your relationships, your routine.

The simulation is not what you need to escape. It's what you came to alchemize.

You are not waiting for life to begin.
You are in it.

This moment is the classroom.
This challenge is the quest.
This breath is the miracle.

Living the remembrance means seeing life not as a distraction from the divine, but as the exact canvas your soul chose to create on. The ordinary *is* the temple. The simulation *is* sacred.

And that includes the messy parts — the anger, the sadness, the breakdowns. Emotional honesty isn't a detour. It's the path. Feeling what's real is how you stay in your **authentic frequency**, even when it hurts. When you feel without shame, you vibrate at truth —

and truth is a high-frequency state.

Sacred Play – Joy as a Frequency Upgrade

Play is a spiritual tuning fork. Often dismissed as childish, it's actually one of the most potent frequency-raising states we have access to. It suspends judgment, quiets the ego, and creates space for spontaneity and joy — which are some of the most healing frequencies available.

Just like a video game rewards creativity, experimentation, and exploration, the simulation rewards play with flow. You become magnetic. Synchronicities increase. Your energy recalibrates not through force — but through fun.

We take healing seriously — but maybe it's time we take joy seriously too. Play isn't just a break from growth — it's a pathway to it.

Play isn't just for children. It's a powerful **frequency-raising state** that dissolves rigidity, opens the heart, and reactivates curiosity. It interrupts the avatar's autopilot loops and brings you back into the Player's creative presence.

Play could be dancing in your kitchen, painting without a plan, playing make-believe, or singing loud in the car. The point isn't what you do — it's how freely you do it.

When you create, explore, laugh, dance, or build something without pressure, you're coding joy into the simulation. That joy becomes medicine — not just for you, but for the collective field. Joy isn't a distraction from healing. It's how your soul remembers who you really are.

The more fun you have, the faster the game upgrades. When you play, you shift timelines not by pushing — but by laughing your way into the next level.

Power-Ups & Portals — Energy Tools That Keep You Aligned

In every well-designed game, power-ups help you stay in the fight, gain new skills, and unlock hidden paths. In the Simulation, energy tools work the same way. They aren't just boosts — they're upgrades that clear the static, recalibrate your field, and anchor your signal.

And portals? Those are the frequency gates — shortcuts that open when your vibration spikes. They can look like a new job, a sudden epiphany, a soul-aligned connection, a turn down an unfamiliar road, or a moment of crystal-clear knowing that you've jumped timelines.

These tools don't just make you feel better. They make you **play better** — more intentional, more attuned, more aligned with the version of you who's already won this level.

Stack them like power-ups. Pairing gratitude with visualization, for example, amplifies both frequencies.

Here are a few of the most effective in-game tools you can activate anytime:

- **Prayer** – Your direct line to the Game Developer (Source). It calms the mind and expands your field.
- **Affirmations** – Subconscious code rewrites. Reprograms your avatar's baseline operating system.
- **Energy Healing** – Clears old data and background static that drains your system.
- **Gratitude** – A frequency amplifier that attracts hidden bonuses and unexpected blessings.
- **Subconscious Reprogramming** – Deep system update. This is how you stop patching and start recoding.

Used consistently, these tools stabilize your vibration and keep your simulation running smoothly. Portals begin to appear — opportunities, intuitive nudges, breakthrough moments that seem to emerge from nowhere.

Don't wait until you're drained to use them. Even five minutes a day can upgrade your access. It's not about doing it all — it's about doing it consistently. These tools keep your avatar sharp, your signal clean, and your access to hidden levels wide open.

Power-ups are how you clear and stabilize.
Portals are how you leap.
Keep both active — and you won't just play the Game.
You'll start to bend it.

Live the Code – What Embodiment Really Looks Like

Living the remembrance doesn't mean being perfect.
It means being **present**.
It means showing up aligned, even when it's messy.
It means letting your values lead, even when it's vulnerable.
It means speaking truth, feeling deeply, and choosing love — even when fear would be easier.

Some days, embodiment means deep service. Other days, it means deep rest.
Some days, it's standing in your power. Other days, it's letting yourself cry.

You're not here to be a brand.
You're here to be real.

Embodiment is what makes your remembrance felt by others.
Not just in what you say — but in how you move, how you love, how you live.

When you embody remembrance, people feel it. You shift rooms, raise vibrations, and give silent permission for others to return to themselves.

That's what makes your light so powerful.
Not because it's loud — but because it's **lived**.

Reflection Prompt

- Where in your life do you still perform instead of embody?
- What simple practices help you stay grounded in your truth?
- How can you bring more play and presence into your daily life?
- What emotion are you avoiding that might be your next portal to growth?
- What has life recently mirrored to you — and what is it teaching you?

Next Level: Boss Level – Recoding the Simulation from the Inside Out

In the next chapter, we'll look at how to fine-tune your inner operating system — so you can align your subconscious, body, and field with the frequency of who you're becoming.

Because you're not just remembering the game.
You're learning how to rewrite it.

CHAPTER 13: BOSS LEVEL – RECODING THE SIMULATION FROM THE INSIDE OUT

You've reached the Boss Level. The part of the Game where old tricks won't save you. Where mindset hacks and surface upgrades stop working.

This isn't about sounding enlightened or downloading better thoughts. It's not about rebooting. It's about **rewriting the system**. Because your avatar is still running on default scripts you didn't choose — programs built from pain, protection, and programming. And now? It's time to recode.

You've remembered who you are — but remembrance isn't the finish line. It's the entry point to deeper transformation. You've felt the shift. You've changed your frequency. But the Boss Level doesn't just test what you *know* — it tests what you **embody**.

When fear returns. When the patterns resurface. When the glitch shows up wearing a new disguise — do you freeze, or do you rewrite the code?

Every trigger is a test. Every reaction is a readout of what's still active in your system.

But this? This is your hidden upgrade. This is where deep recoding begins — where you stop reacting and start rewriting the simulation from the inside out.

In this chapter, you won't just understand the map. You'll learn how to become the player who rewrites it.

Behind the Scenes – Your Subconscious Is Running the Show

Most of your thoughts and actions don't come from conscious choice — they come from subconscious patterns. And those patterns don't just influence how you think — they literally shape how the simulation renders around you.

Your subconscious is like a 24/7 radio tower, quietly broadcasting your deepest beliefs — even the ones you didn't choose. It doesn't stream what you want — it streams what you believe. And the simulation plays back that signal in real time. If you believe you're not safe, worthy, seen, or powerful — those frequencies will generate a simulation that reflects those beliefs as reality. Not because it's true, but because it's been coded that way in your system — like playing Level One with a cracked headset and laggy controls.

Most of this coding happens between ages 0–7 (your avatar's base programming phase), when you were absorbing beliefs from your family, culture, religion, and early experiences. Maybe you were told to be quiet. Maybe you felt unsafe, or invisible, or only loved when you performed. Those messages didn't just shape your childhood — they shaped your code. These beliefs are often invisible, but they influence everything — from how you handle conflict to whether you pursue your dreams.

Here's the key: **your simulation doesn't respond to what you want — it responds to what you believe.**

It's not that positive thinking is useless — it's just incomplete. Until you shift the subconscious signal, the simulation can't stabilize the new settings. Deep subconscious transformation isn't about just thinking positively. It's about shifting the subconscious signal your avatar is emitting so it aligns with your Higher Self. It works at the intersection of:

- Subconscious belief reprogramming
- Somatic (body-based) healing
- Nervous system regulation
- Energetic alignment

It doesn't just rewrite the narrative. It rewires the energetic and emotional infrastructure that narrative is built on.

This is the technology of transformation.

This is how you stop reacting from old wounds — and start creating from new awareness.

Checkpoint Prompt

What patterns keep pulling you back into old levels — even when you've outgrown them?

Patch Notes — How to Spot Old Code Still Running

(These are your debug alerts in disguise.)

Old code doesn't always show up as obvious dysfunction. Often, it masquerades as overthinking, people-pleasing, indecision, or self-sabotage. It hides behind habits you justify, relationships you tolerate, and emotions you suppress.

Here are some signs that your avatar is still running on outdated programming:

- 🔁 **Glitch Loop:** You attract the same relationships, dynamics, or disappointments over and over, even in different packaging.
- 🚧 **Blocked Upgrade:** You feel like you "know" what to do but can't seem to follow through — you're stuck between insight and embodiment.

- 🐱 **Mask Mode:** You base your decisions on avoiding judgment, abandonment, or conflict instead of honoring your truth.
- ☠️ **Fear Reflex:** You default to fear, even when there's no threat — your nervous system can't tell the difference between now and the original wound.
- ⚫ **Sabotage Spike:** You self-sabotage when things start going well, unconsciously reinforcing the belief that success isn't safe or sustainable.
- ‖ **Pause Over Presence:** You hit pause or mute when discomfort arises, rather than decoding the message hidden inside the discomfort.
- ⌛ **Stuck Loading Screen:** You feel like you've outgrown parts of your life — but feel too scared, guilty, or unworthy to move forward.

You're not broken — you're just running an old patch.

And the good news? You're the programmer. The code can be rewritten. The game will update the moment you do.

When you update the belief, regulate the nervous system, and shift the energetic signal, the simulation must respond. Not because you forced it — but because you leveled up. And once your signal shifts, the simulation has no choice but to load a new version of the game.

Autopilot Override – Dismantling the NPC Within

You can set intentions, script your affirmations, and visualize your dream reality —
but if your subconscious is still running outdated code, you're not the one driving.

You're watching the **NPC (non-playable character)** version of yourself go through the motions — repeating patterns, playing safe, avoiding upgrades.
It's not sabotage. It's autopilot.

Your subconscious is like your avatar's internal GPS. It was programmed in early life — learning how to respond to fear, failure, rejection, and love.
But it hasn't updated the route since then.

That's why, even after a spiritual awakening, you might still:

- React in ways that feel old
- Choose what's familiar over what's aligned
- Delay change even when you *say* you're ready

 ✦ **The simulation doesn't respond to what you want — it responds to the code you're running.**

So if you're still looping through the same missions...
It's time to **override autopilot** and return control to your Higher Self.

This is where **subconscious reprogramming** comes in.

174

It's the difference between watching the game play itself...
And grabbing the controller.

The Reprogramming Protocol – A New Blueprint for Transformation

If the Real-Time Reprogramming in Chapter 6 is your quick, in-the-moment reset, this protocol is your full system upgrade — designed to decode, upgrade, and rewire the deeper beliefs shaping your reality.

You've already learned how to observe and shift your beliefs in real time. Now, you're stepping into the full method — a rhythm for transformation you can return to any time a pattern feels persistent, painful, or outdated.

There's no one-size-fits-all path to healing — but there is a repeatable rhythm: **observe, feel, challenge, rewire, and embody.** This process isn't linear. It's layered. Some patterns peel easily; others arrive in spirals. You may revisit the same wound more than once, but every loop brings more truth, clarity, and freedom.

This isn't about fixing yourself — it's about freeing yourself. You're not broken. You're coded.

This is how you reprogram the game from within — one belief at a time.

The 5-Step Rewiring Protocol

Observe → Feel → Challenge → Rewire → Embody

1. **Observe – Identify the Trigger & Root Belief**

   ✦ Ask yourself: *"What is happening right now that I want to change?"*

This could be a reaction, emotion, behavior, or situation that keeps repeating — something that feels off, painful, or misaligned.

- What triggered me just now?
- What emotion or thought came up?
- Where do I feel stuck or limited?

Once you spot the surface reaction, go deeper:

"What belief might be causing this?"

Is it a fear of rejection? A story that you're not good enough? An old program that says success isn't safe?

<u>*Name the trigger & the belief underneath it.*</u> That's how you bring the pattern into the light and begin to change it.

Every awareness is a doorway to reprogramming.

2. **Feel it Fully – Unlock the Stored Emotion**

Your body holds what your mind avoids. When a belief gets installed, it's paired with an emotional imprint.

Tune into where you feel it. Is it tightness in the chest? A knot in the stomach? Heat in the face? Numbness in the limbs? You don't need a dramatic breakdown for it to matter. Feelings like disappointment, loneliness, or irritation carry just as much wisdom.

Let the sensation be felt instead of fixed. You're not broken — you're processing.

If you feel overwhelmed, pause and return when you're grounded. Healing happens at the pace of safety.

3. **Challenge the Belief – Listen Without Judgment**

Now that you've felt the emotion, it's time to meet the part of you that formed this belief.

Ask the reaction or sensation:

"What are you trying to protect me from?"

Most limiting beliefs were born as survival strategies. Even self-sabotage is often self-protection in disguise.

Ask deeper questions like:

- *What are you afraid will happen if we let go of this belief?*
- *How old is the part of me that believes this?*
- *What was I taught or shown that made this feel true?*
- *What do you wish I had known back then?*
- *What do you need now to feel safe enough to let this go?*

177

For example, let's say you keep putting off launching your project. On the surface, it might look like laziness or procrastination. But when you check in, you realize the belief underneath is: *"If I fail, I'll disappoint everyone."* That part of you might be trying to protect you from shame — because at one point, failure didn't just hurt, it felt unsafe.

Remember — this isn't about proving the belief wrong with logic. It's about understanding the need behind it. Every belief was created to help you adapt and keep you safe. That made it necessary back then, even if it's no longer true.

Meet the belief with compassion, not correction.
This is how you create the safety required for transformation.

4. Rewire the Belief – Update the Mental Blueprint

Now that you've met the belief and understood its original purpose, it's time to install an upgraded version — one that aligns with who you're becoming.

Rewiring isn't just about thinking differently. It's about **re-teaching your body, mind, and energy** what's safe, true, and possible.

Here are powerful ways to reprogram the subconscious:

- **Affirmations** – Speak phrases that feel true in your body, not just in your mind. Use language that activates emotion and resonance, like "I am safe now" or "It's okay to receive." Repetition isn't enough — *belief* must be felt.

- **Visualization** – Picture yourself already living this new belief. What do you see, hear, feel, and do? Engage all senses. The more vividly you imagine it, the more your subconscious accepts it as real.

- **Somatic techniques** – Include breathwork, movement, or touch-based practices like placing a hand over your heart while repeating the new belief. These send safety signals to your nervous system, helping your body embody the shift.

- **EFT (Emotional Freedom Techniques)** – Also known as "tapping," this technique involves gently tapping on meridian points while focusing on a memory, belief, or emotion. It helps reduce intensity, release stuck energy, and reprogram the nervous system.

- **Subconscious Reprogramming** – Install new beliefs in a relaxed, receptive state. This can be done through self-practices like hypnosis, meditation, or repetition — or with the guidance of a practitioner. Modalities such as Quantum Reprogramming™, EMDR (Eye Movement Desensitization and Reprocessing), NLP (Neuro-Linguistic Programming), or energy healing can accelerate the process by shifting the core subconscious imprint.

All of these methods work differently, but they share the same goal: **to bring your autopilot into alignment with your soul.** Because when your subconscious and Higher Self are on the same page, the simulation doesn't stand a chance. That's the real cheat code — not because it skips the work, but because it dissolves the static that was slowing you down. You're not just remembering who you are — you're upgrading into it.

5. Anchor with Aligned Action – Sync Energy + Embodiment

You've done the inner rewiring — now it's time to live like it.

Thoughts are powerful. Emotions fuel change. But aligned action is the code the simulation responds to. It's not enough to think differently — you have to move differently. That's what signals the Game to load a new version of reality.

Ask yourself:

What would someone with this new belief do?

- ☐ Speak up in a meeting
- ☐ Rest without guilt
- ☐ Accept support
- ☐ Say no
- ☐ Post the thing
- ☐ Show up before you feel "ready"

Even tiny shifts — done consistently — tell your system, "This is safe now."

This is where many people get stuck. They do the healing, feel the shift... but keep acting like the old version of themselves. Not because they failed — because their nervous system hasn't caught up. Habit is just old code looping in the background.

To rewrite the field, **your frequency and your actions must align.** That's when the simulation recognizes the upgrade — not just in thought, but in being. That's when the pixels shift. The room changes. New opportunities appear.

And no — it won't always be perfect. You'll revert sometimes. That's okay. Reprogramming is a practice of **consistent pattern interruption.**

Every time you act in alignment with the new code, you override the old loop. Every time you choose the upgraded path, the field updates. That's how you shift the Game — not by force, but by embodiment.

You're not just rethinking your life. **You're becoming the update.**

Reprogramming isn't about perfection — it's about consistent pattern interruption. Every time you choose differently, you override the old frequency and shift the version of the Game that loads around you.

Reflection Prompt

- What pattern or belief do you keep repeating — even though you "know better"?
- Where in your life do you feel stuck between your truth and your reactions?
- What would your life look like if your nervous system felt safe being fully you?

Next Level: Bonus Level — Beyond the Rules of the Game

Ready for the Bonus Round?

You've dismantled the autopilot, upgraded your emotional code, and learned to sync energy with action. But what if there's more waiting just beyond the rules you thought were fixed?

In the next chapter, we step into the **Bonus Level** — where synchronicity accelerates, reality bends faster, and the Game starts responding to your soul's frequency in real-time.

Let's explore what becomes possible when you no longer play by the old code — because now, **you're playing as the Creator.**

CHAPTER 14: BONUS LEVEL – BEYOND THE RULES OF THE GAME

Welcome to the bonus level — the stage that unlocks after you've completed the main quest. You've already unlocked the big secrets, passed the major checkpoints, and mastered the core mechanics. But now? You're not just playing the game — you're shaping it.

Not everyone reaches it — but if you've made it here, chances are, your soul signed up for more than just healing. You came to test the edges of the code. To see what becomes possible when you move in total alignment with your soul frequency.

Everything you've learned so far — about frequency, beliefs, levels, and the Higher Self — becomes your foundation here. But now, you're entering a phase where you get to play beyond the rules, not just within them. This is where the edges of what's "real" start to blur, and your potential becomes more experiential than theoretical.

At the Master Levels, you begin to experiment with bending the simulation itself. You've already shifted timelines, rewritten beliefs, and built a relationship with your Higher Self. Now, the question becomes:

What else can you do that the old rules say is impossible?

Throughout history and across cultures, certain avatars have cracked open the deeper mechanics of this simulation — proving what's possible when you move beyond the default settings.

Healing Hacks — Rewriting the Body with Belief

At the Boss Level, healing isn't something done *to* you — it's something activated *by* you. The nervous system, subconscious beliefs, and emotional trauma all impact the body's ability to regenerate. Many people have reversed chronic illness, reduced pain, or accelerated healing through breathwork, visualization, somatic regulation, belief reprogramming, and energetic clearing.

Take, for example, Dr. Joe Dispenza — whose personal story of healing a shattered spine through focused meditation and visualization sparked a global movement. Thousands of his workshop participants have reported spontaneous remissions, improved mobility, reduced pain, and even the reversal of so-called "incurable" conditions. These transformations didn't come from pills or procedures, but from a rewired internal network — where thought and energy reshaped biology.

Another example is Anita Moorjani, who documented her near-death experience and miraculous cancer remission in her book *Dying to Be Me*. Her insights highlight how releasing fear, aligning with love, and remembering the body's innate intelligence can initiate profound physical transformation.

Research into the placebo effect continues to support this idea: when a person truly believes they are receiving healing, the body often responds as if it were — because the subconscious and nervous system have been given a new directive.

This isn't magical thinking. It's neurobiology, energy medicine, and consciousness at work. When you shift your belief system, regulate your emotional state, and enter elevated frequencies like gratitude and love, your body begins to reroute energy for healing.

The simulation follows energetic commands. When your beliefs, emotions, and focus align, you're not just hoping for healing — you're coding it into the system.

You are the healer. Your mind is the script. Your energy is the signal. Your body simply follows the code.

This is the next phase of medicine: one where your energy field becomes the prescription, and your consciousness is the catalyst. You don't need to wait for permission — you already have the power.

Rule-Breaking Mode – Defying the Default Settings

Some avatars access abilities that seem to defy physical law: levitation, telekinesis, psychic intuition, breath control that halts biological responses, or heat manipulation.

These "superpowers" are rare not because they're impossible, but because most people never reach the level of alignment, belief, and mental discipline required to unlock them. Children often demonstrate latent abilities — like seeing energy fields or accessing past-life memories — before they're trained out of it by societal programming.

Examples of case files from the edge of the simulation are below of what becomes possible when we move beyond default human programming.

🦋 Examples of Superhuman Abilities Across Cultures and Research

- **Levitation**: Mystics like St. Joseph of Cupertino reportedly lifted off the ground during spiritual ecstasy — witnessed by large crowds and documented across religious texts.

- **Heat Generation**: Tibetan monks practicing Tummo meditation raise body temperature in freezing conditions using only breath and intention — confirmed by Harvard studies.

- **Extreme Cold Resistance**: Wim Hof ("The Iceman") uses breathwork to control immune response and endure freezing temperatures — scientifically documented.

- **Pain Tolerance & Energy Projection**: Shaolin monks perform feats of endurance, physical mastery, and chi manipulation through focused training.

- **Remote Viewing**: Participants in the CIA's Stargate Project accessed distant locations psychically, contributing to military intel without physical contact.

- **Electromagnetic Field Coherence**: HeartMath Institute research shows how emotions like gratitude alter the body's energy field and influence others.

- **Mind-Body Healing**: Placebo & Nocebo effects demonstrate how belief alone can create healing — or harm — proving mind-over-biology principles.

- **Blindfolded Perception**: Children in midbrain activation programs have demonstrated the ability to read and navigate while blindfolded, using extrasensory perception.

These are just a few examples that reveal that the simulation has hidden mechanics — ones that become accessible through belief, discipline, and energetic coherence. They point to the possibility that what we call "natural law" is more flexible than we've been taught, and that those willing to unlearn their limits might just find themselves rewriting them.

Whether you see these as anomalies, spiritual gifts, or future science, the fact remains: the rules of this game bend further than we think.

189

These aren't just outliers or miracles. They're invitations. Previews of what the human operating system is truly capable of — once we uninstall the belief that we're limited.

You're not just bending reality — you're finally remembering how fluid it always was.

The Bonus Level isn't about becoming superhuman. It's about remembering you were never just human to begin with.

Sensory Glitch – Seeing Beyond the Avatar

In the last section, we explored rare superhuman abilities — but what if some of these gifts aren't rare at all? What if they're dormant in most of us, quietly waiting to be reactivated?

What if your senses aren't the source of perception, but simply filters — narrow channels through which your avatar receives a limited version of reality?

This idea might sound radical, but growing evidence and real-world demonstrations suggest it's already happening — especially in children. Across the globe, young people have shown abilities that challenge our current understanding of how the senses work.

In experiments often dismissed by mainstream science, children have been observed identifying colors, reading books, and navigating rooms while wearing opaque eye masks. These aren't just magic tricks — they're documented demonstrations that question the assumption that vision is purely optical.

One example comes from the phenomenon known as "midbrain activation" or "blindfold reading," where children are trained to "see" while their eyes are fully covered. Programs across Europe, Russia, India, and Asia have reported kids accurately naming shapes, colors, and even reading text — without using their physical eyes. While controversial, neurological studies of these children show increased alpha and theta brainwave activity — states linked with intuition, heightened perception, and access to non-local information.

This hints at a much deeper truth: **what if vision is actually frequency recognition — and your brain is interpreting information from energetic fields, not just photons hitting your retina?**

Researchers like Dr. Dean Radin and the Institute of Noetic Sciences have proposed that consciousness might be more field-based than brain-based. If your avatar is actually a bioenergetic receiver, then what you call "sight" might be just one way you're decoding the quantum field — not the only one.

And it's not just kids. Have you ever felt someone staring at you... without seeing them? Or known who was calling before you looked? These subtle experiences suggest that you're already picking up on more than meets the eye. You've just been trained to ignore it.

Children, especially between ages 5–12, seem to remain more attuned to subtle frequencies before the conditioning of logic and visual dominance takes over. What appears as a "glitch" in the system may actually be a glimpse of your original blueprint — before programming told you what was real and what wasn't.

These aren't just anomalies — they're evidence that your avatar was always built for more. With trust, training, and a willingness to remember, you can begin to access perceptual channels that go far beyond your five physical senses.

The question isn't *if* you have these abilities.

The question is: **are you ready to remember them?**

Multiplayer Mind – Consciousness Across Dimensions

Imagine a glowing web of light connecting every person, plant, animal, and particle — your consciousness is one node in this infinite network. When you think, feel, or focus, you send out ripples that influence the entire system.

As you begin to unlock higher sensory channels within yourself, another realization emerges: **you're not evolving alone**. The more you tune your frequency, the more you begin to sense others playing at this level too.

This is where the simulation upgrades into a new mode: **Multiplayer Mind**.

Once you begin playing at the Multiplayer level, it becomes clear — your consciousness isn't just housed in your brain. It extends into the Field — a web of information, emotion, energy, and intelligence that connects all living beings. Your awareness flows through this entire system and interfaces with your environment like a multidimensional antenna.

This expanded consciousness enables abilities like remote viewing, where individuals receive impressions of people or locations from a distance without physical interaction. The U.S. military's Stargate Project studied remote viewing for over 20 years — where participants accurately described people, places, or events far away without any physical contact. Their minds accessed information beyond the five senses, hinting at how consciousness can travel without the body.

You may also begin to notice more frequent telepathic moments — thinking about someone before they call, or intuitively sensing someone's mood before they speak. These aren't coincidences. They're demonstrations of entangled consciousness and shared fields of awareness.

When you meditate with a group, you may feel the energy intensify. Heart coherence studies from the HeartMath Institute show that when multiple individuals align their emotional and energetic fields, they create a measurable impact on one another — and even on the environment around them.

In these expanded states, subtle cues begin to speak louder. Symbols carry deeper meanings. Dreams reveal instructions. Thoughts may "drop in" rather than be consciously generated. These are signs your consciousness is operating within a larger intelligence system — connected to something beyond you, yet part of you.

And as this network strengthens, you realize you're not just upgrading your personal reality — you're editing the game code across timelines.

As you heal in one version of reality, that transformation sends ripples across dimensions — affecting parallel versions of you in other lifetimes or timelines. Every belief you rewrite, every wound you transmute, liberates another "you" still playing at that level. Healing becomes holographic, not linear.

You also begin to clear energetic debris from ancestral lines and past lives. Your inner work frees trapped energy — breaking generational trauma, karmic loops, and soul contracts. You're not just healing your life — you're liberating entire timelines.

At this point, you may even start to feel like you're coordinating with your Higher Self — making moves on the bigger Game board. You'll sense when to show up in someone's life, when to exit, when to pause, and when to act — not from logic, but from a knowing that comes from a map you're starting to remember.

The simulation becomes more transparent. The veil gets thinner. Miracles become measurable — not magic tricks, but upgrades made possible because you've learned how to play with a deeper layer of the simulation's code.

You Are the Update – Becoming the Patch Note

Master Levels aren't about status. They're about soul alignment, energetic transmission, and quiet revolution. At this point in the game, your presence alone begins to shift the field around you — not because you're doing more, but because you're aligned more deeply with your soul's truth.

You're not here to fit the old paradigm — you're here to upgrade it from within.

You are the walking upgrade — an update encoded in human form. Every time you embody a higher frequency, every time you choose alignment over fear, or love over judgment, you anchor a new potential into the shared simulation.

⚡ Embodiment in Action:

- Healing your body in ways that challenge what others thought was possible — showing them it is.
- Experiencing time differently — completing in an hour what used to take a day — because you're operating from flow instead of force.
- Sharing ideas, art, or words that seem to activate something deep in others — like a soul memory being awakened.
- Walking into a room and shifting the energy without saying a word — because your frequency speaks louder than your voice.
- Saying no without guilt and yes without fear — honoring your truth in every choice.
- Laughing, dancing, or resting unapologetically — because joy, stillness, and pleasure are part of your power.

You're not chasing the next level. You are the next level.

Living as the update means you stop needing validation. You don't need everyone to understand. You just live it. Breathe it. Let your life become the transmission.

It might look like using your voice in new ways — breaking cycles of silence or emotional suppression with one conscious breath. Or choosing to build a business that prioritizes healing over hustle, authenticity over algorithms. It's not always loud or visible. Often, the most revolutionary upgrades happen quietly, in the way you choose to live each moment differently.

In this space, synchronicities are constant. Miracles feel normal. People come to you not because you marketed to them — but because your frequency called them in. You're not here to convince. You're here to be.

Living your truth also means honoring how *you* move through the simulation. And for some, that update is even hardwired into their system.

✳ The Neurodivergent Frequency

Some souls are born with unique wiring — what the world might label as neurodivergent. These individuals often feel more, sense more, and think differently. They may process time and emotion in nonlinear ways, move between ideas like timelines, or experience intense sensitivity to energy and environment.

In the simulation, this isn't a flaw. It's a feature.

Neurodivergent traits often point to a higher sensitivity to the field — a deeper awareness of unseen layers. These souls came in carrying a different version of the code. They might appear 'out of sync' with the old systems, but they're actually designed to help rewrite them.

You might feel like **you're running new software on old hardware** — like your operating system is too advanced for the density of the current world. Glitchy, laggy, misread. But that's not because there's something wrong with you. It's because you're built to upgrade the whole environment.

You came equipped with strange "patch notes" in your code —

updates that don't match the current program, but are meant to rebuild it from the inside out.

Your sensitivity is not a weakness — it's part of your soul's mission. You are not here to fit the old paradigm.

You are here to evolve it.

So yes, you can bend time. Rewrite biology. Break inherited patterns.
Tune into quantum wisdom.
But not because you're special. But because you remembered.

You don't need to believe it all. Just stay curious.
The Master Levels don't require certainty — just willingness.

You are not waiting for a savior.
You are the upgrade.

You're not here to dim down — you're here to restore full-spectrum human potential.

And you didn't come to play by the rules.
You came to rewrite them.

Now it's time to zoom all the way out.
Not to escape the Game — but to see it clearly.

The simulation was never outside of you.
It's *you* — your frequency, your memories, your evolution — rendered into experience.

You're not just a Player anymore.
You are the Game.

Reflection Prompts

- What shift happens in your life when you stop chasing validation and start trusting your vibration?
- Where are you still waiting for permission to be who you already are?
- What part of your life could become an upgrade for others just by you living it more consciously?
- How might your "differences" be the exact design required to bring in the new system?
- What would it mean to move through life as a walking update, rather than a problem to fix?

Epilogue: You Are the Game

The simulation doesn't just respond to what you think.
It responds to what you are.

In the final section, we'll zoom out one last time — to remember why this Game exists, and how your evolution shapes not just your world, but ours.

Because in every pixel, in every timeline, in every breath — the player, the avatar, and the code are all you.

EPILOGUE:
YOU ARE THE GAME

You've reached the edge of the map — only to realize... the map was never fixed. It expands with you.

Because this Game was never about winning.
It was about **remembering**.

Remembering that you're more than your thoughts.
More than your trauma.
More than your avatar.

You're the Player.
The code.
The entire simulation.

Every belief, every choice, every frequency shift — you wrote it. And you can rewrite it.

The Beginning Hidden in the Ending

If this book opened something in you — a new thought, a softening, a spark — then it did its job. Not to give you answers, but to remind you of what you already know.

That you're powerful.
That you're not broken.
That you're part of something far bigger — and far more beautiful — than you've ever been told.

You don't have to be perfect.
You don't have to rush.
You just have to stay awake.

Because now, you know the truth:

That reality is responsive.

That the Field is listening.

That every thought, every belief, every feeling matters.

This isn't about chasing some future version of yourself. It's about tuning into the version that's already aligned — already encoded in your frequency.

You're not here to figure it all out — you're here to *play with remembering*. To explore your truth, not solve it. To treat your growth like a sacred experiment. To let curiosity lead you deeper into your own design.

Keep noticing.
Keep feeling.
Keep choosing.

You don't have to do it all at once.
You just have to do it one moment at a time.

The more aligned you become with your soul's signal, the more the simulation will shift around you to reflect that alignment. That's not magic. That's just how the field works.

You Are the Update

When you heal, you change the code.
When you love, you stabilize the field.
When you embody truth, you open levels.

You're not just moving through the game.
You're evolving it.

Every internal shift you make — every belief you rewire, every emotion you process, every old pattern you interrupt — creates a ripple in the collective simulation. Your frequency doesn't just affect your personal reality. It impacts the whole system.

That's why your healing isn't selfish.
It's sacred.

You are the living patch note in a cosmic update. Every time you align more fully with your truth, you upgrade the human experience

— for yourself, and for everyone around you.

So if it ever feels hard, remember this:
You chose to be here.
You chose this avatar.
You chose this version of Earth, this level, this time.

Not as punishment.
But because you're ready.

You are the bridge between Source and self.
Between remembering and becoming.
Between what was and what's possible next.

So go play.
Go love.
Go create.
Go rewrite what's been waiting to be rewritten.

You are the Game. The Code is Love. And the Controller? It's been in your hands the whole time.

This is how we heal — by remembering the truth beneath the programming. By taking back authorship of our frequency. By learning how to play the game as the version of ourselves we came here to be.

Supporting References

The ideas in *The Game of Remembrance* were channeled through personal experience, intuitive insight, and lived transformation. While the content wasn't derived from external sources, the following works across science, psychology, mysticism, philosophy, and energy healing offer supportive perspectives that resonate with the principles explored throughout the book. They are shared here for readers who wish to dive deeper into these themes from multiple angles.

Scientific Support

Bohr, N. (1934). *Atomic Theory and the Description of Nature.* Cambridge University Press.

Bohm, D. (1980). *Wholeness and the Implicate Order.* Routledge.

Einstein, A. (1954). *Ideas and Opinions.* Crown Publishers.

Feynman, R. P., Leighton, R. B., & Sands, M. (1965). *The Feynman Lectures on Physics, Vol. 3: Quantum Mechanics*. Addison-Wesley.

Goswami, A. (1995). *The Self-Aware Universe: How Consciousness Creates the Material World*. TarcherPerigee.

Greene, B. (2004). *The Fabric of the Cosmos: Space, Time, and the Texture of Reality*. Vintage.

HeartMath Institute. (n.d.). *Research Library*. Retrieved from https://www.heartmath.org

Heisenberg, W. (1958). *Physics and Philosophy: The Revolution in Modern Science*. Harper.

Hof, W. (2020). *The Wim Hof Method: Activate Your Full Human Potential*. Sounds True.

Pribram, K. H. (1991). *Brain and Perception: Holonomy and Structure in Figural Processing*. Lawrence Erlbaum Associates.

Radin, D. (2006). *Entangled Minds: Extrasensory Experiences in a Quantum Reality*. Paraview Pocket Books.

Sheldrake, R. (1988). *The Presence of the Past: Morphic Resonance and the Habits of Nature*. Vintage.

Tesla, N. (n.d.). "If you want to find the secrets of the universe, think in terms of energy, frequency and vibration." (Quote attributed)

Wheeler, J. A., & Zurek, W. H. (1983). *Quantum Theory and Measurement*. Princeton University Press.

Psychological Insights

Hawkins, D. R. (1995). *Power vs. Force: The Hidden Determinants of Human Behavior*. Hay House.

Jung, C. G. (1969). *The Archetypes and the Collective Unconscious*. Princeton University Press.

Levine, P. A. (1997). *Waking the Tiger: Healing Trauma*. North Atlantic Books.

Maté, G. (2011). *When the Body Says No: The Cost of Hidden Stress*. Vintage Canada.

Spiritual Wisdom & Soul Exploration

Abraham-Hicks (2004). *Ask and It Is Given*. Hay House.

Cannon, D. (2003). *The Convoluted Universe (Vol. 1)*. Ozark Mountain Publishing.

Goddard, N. (1952). *The Power of Awareness*. Martino Publishing.

Newton, M. (1994). *Journey of Souls: Case Studies of Life Between Lives*. Llewellyn Publications.

Roberts, J. (1972). *Seth Speaks: The Eternal Validity of the Soul*. Amber-Allen Publishing.

Yogananda, P. (1946). *Autobiography of a Yogi*. Self-Realization Fellowship.

Conscious Creation & Energy Work

Abraham-Hicks (2004). *Ask and It Is Given.* Hay House.

Braden, G. (2007). *The Divine Matrix: Bridging Time, Space, Miracles, and Belief.* Hay House.

Dispenza, J. (2017). *Becoming Supernatural: How Common People Are Doing the Uncommon.* Hay House.

Lipton, B. H. (2005). *The Biology of Belief: Unleashing the Power of Consciousness, Matter & Miracles.* Hay House.

Watts, A. (1957). *The Way of Zen.* Pantheon Books.

Author's Note:

The works listed here didn't inspire or create this book — they're shared as examples of how similar truths show up across different fields. These are just a few references out of many that echo what's written here. You're encouraged to explore what resonates, stay curious, and trust your own inner guidance most of all.

Glossary of Terms

Akashic Field

A multidimensional field of information that holds the vibrational record of every thought, action, and soul journey across time and space. Think of it as the spiritual iCloud or memory bank of the universe.

Autopilot (NPC Mode)

A default state where you're running on subconscious programming — reacting, repeating, and moving through life without conscious choice. Like an NPC in a game, you follow the script instead of creating it.

Avatar

The temporary identity or human version of you operating within the simulation. Your avatar is influenced by programming, conditioning, and subconscious patterns.

Awakening

The process of remembering your divine nature and seeing beyond the illusions of the simulation. Often triggered by trauma, loss, or spiritual insight.

Belief

An internal program that sets the frequency you operate from, shaping what you attract and how you interpret the game around you.

Boss

A major challenge at the end of a level that tests your growth and skills. In this game, the boss might be a belief, pattern, or old version of you that must be faced to level up.

Brainwaves (Theta, Alpha, Beta)

Different frequencies of brain activity. Theta (ages 0–7) is deeply programmable. Alpha (8–14) is relaxed and imaginative. Beta (15+) is alert, logical, and externally focused.

Collective Field

The energetic environment created by the combined thoughts, emotions, and frequencies of all beings. This field impacts and is impacted by individual and group consciousness.

Consciousness

The awareness and intelligence behind all life, often associated with soul, energy, or the field.

Download
A sudden influx of insight or intuitive knowing, often perceived as coming from a higher source.

Ego
The personality-based identity shaped by conditioning. Originally designed as an internal alert system to keep you safe, it often becomes overprotective — limiting your true self-expression and keeping you in familiar patterns.

Embodiment
Living your remembrance by aligning your actions, emotions, and energy with your highest self. It's the practice of becoming what you believe.

Emotional Code
A recurring emotional imprint that acts like software in your subconscious. Often formed through early life events or ancestral patterns, emotional codes can be rewritten through awareness, reprogramming, and healing.

Energetic Hygiene
The intentional practice of clearing, protecting, and grounding your energy. This may include smudging, salt baths, breathwork, visualization, energy healing, or disconnecting from chaotic environments.

Energy
The creative force that flows through everything, building your reality based on the frequency you're tuned to.

Energy Healing

Modalities (like Reiki) that clear, balance, or align the subtle energetic body to support physical, emotional, and spiritual well-being.

Field

The energetic space that connects all things; often refers to the quantum or unified field of consciousness.

Frequency

The vibrational signature of your current state. It determines what levels, people, and experiences you align with.

Glitch

A disruption in your energetic or mental pattern, often a sign of misalignment or unintegrated programming.

Higher Self

The eternal, wise part of your consciousness that guides your soul's journey. Often experienced as intuition, inspiration, or knowing.

Intuition

Inner knowing or guidance that bypasses logic and comes from the soul or higher self (higher consciousness).

Level (*some use Timeline*)

A version of reality aligned with a particular frequency or set of beliefs. As your inner world shifts, you shift levels (timeline).

Masks

The roles, identities, and coping mechanisms your avatar develops to stay safe or accepted in early life. Healing often involves removing these masks to access your authentic self.

Multi-Frequency Simulation Theory

The foundational concept of this book: reality is a simulation responsive to your frequency. You are constantly shifting levels and versions of reality based on your inner state.

Observer

The neutral part of you that witnesses without reacting. The Observer allows you to step out of programming and into conscious response. It is the bridge between the avatar and the Player.

Player

Your true self — the conscious observer and soul navigating the simulation through the avatar. The Player can zoom out, guide, and choose with awareness.

Programming

Subconscious beliefs and emotional codes installed in early life, often through repetition, trauma, or inherited patterns. Programming defines how your avatar reacts to life.

Quantum Physics

The science of how energy behaves at the smallest levels. It shows reality is made of vibration, influenced by observation, and shaped by unseen fields — revealing that your beliefs and emotions help shape the version of the game you experience.

Quantum Reprogramming™

Joann's signature healing method that combines subconscious rewiring, energy work, and belief transformation to help individuals rapidly align with their true self.

Remembrance

The experience of reconnecting to your divine essence and realizing the simulation is a tool for soul growth. Living in remembrance is the goal of the game.

Sacred Neutrality

A state of non-judgmental awareness where you see experiences and people not as good or bad, but as part of a greater unfolding. This lens helps you stay out of ego loops and access higher perspective.

Sacred Play

Engaging with life from a place of joy, curiosity, and creative expression. Sacred play dissolves resistance and raises your frequency, helping you access deeper alignment and flow in the simulation. A combination of your thoughts, feelings, actions, and nervous system regulation.

Shadow Work

The process of exploring, integrating, and healing the hidden or suppressed aspects of yourself (your "shadow"). Shadow work helps reveal the unconscious wounds and patterns that limit your frequency and shape your avatar's default behaviors.

Side Quests

Optional experiences your soul chooses for growth, joy, healing, or service. These may include art, travel, creative projects, or relationships that enhance your journey but aren't your main soul mission.

Simulation

The energetic, frequency-based construct we experience as reality. It's not fake — it's malleable. Like a video game, it's coded with rules but responsive to the Player and avatar.

Soul Contracts

Agreements made between souls before incarnation to help each other learn specific lessons or evolve through particular experiences.

Soul Mission

The overarching purpose or lesson your soul chose to explore in this lifetime. While it may evolve, your soul mission is often linked to healing, service, expression, or transformation.

Subconscious

The part of the mind that stores your automatic beliefs, responses, and patterns. It runs most of your avatar's programming until intentionally reprogrammed.

Torus Field

The donut-shaped energy field generated by the heart and body. It flows in a looping pattern, circulating energy inward and outward. Your torus field is how your frequency is broadcast into the simulation, influencing what you attract and experience.

Triggers

Emotional reactions or activations that reveal unresolved wounds, programming, or unmet needs. Triggers are portals to healing and remembrance.

Vibration

The emotional and energetic resonance you emit, which shapes your reality.

About the Author

Joann Marchese is an internationally published author, visionary mindset coach, Reiki Master, and the creator of **Quantum Reprogramming**™ — a groundbreaking method that merges neuroscience, energy healing, and spiritual psychology to rewire the subconscious and realign individuals with their soul's highest level (timeline).

She is the founder of **Infinite Mindset Coaching**, a transformative brand dedicated to helping purpose-driven souls break free from emotional conditioning, release limiting beliefs, and step into heart-led, frequency-aligned living. Through private in person or virtual coaching, guided journals, and immersive healing tools, Joann empowers others to consciously code the life they were born to live.

Her spiritual gifts awakened further after the death of her husband Jack — a profound turning point that opened the door to multidimensional visions and a new way of living rooted in remembrance, not suffering.

Joann's work has been recognized for its depth and impact. She was personally invited by self-help leaders Jim Britt and Jim Lutes to contribute to *The Change Book Series* (Vol. 23), and has been featured in magazines and on podcasts exploring healing, consciousness, and transformation. She also created the *Infinite Mindset* YouTube channel — a space for expanding awareness and reclaiming inner power.

When she's not coaching or creating, Joann is usually immersed in nature, channeling art, or laughing with her husband John and their beautifully blended family.

Free Your Mind Elevate Your Life

Take the Work Deeper

Transform insight into embodiment.

Whether you're ready to anchor your shifts, reprogram your beliefs, or track your vibrational growth—guided journals and personalized coaching can help you elevate faster and integrate deeper.

The Yin-Yang Harmony Journals

Butterfly Goddess Edition & Pride & Joy Edition

These beautifully designed journals guide you in cultivating balance, self-love, and emotional clarity. Featuring daily prompts, reflection questions, and empowering mindset shifts, each edition offers a unique visual style while delivering the same powerful framework for growth. They can be easily purchased through Amazon.

SCAN TO EXPLORE

Personalized 1 on 1 Coaching

Infinite Mindset Coaching

Joann Marchese blends neuroscience, energy healing, and spiritual psychology in her signature method, *Quantum Reprogramming*™, to help you:

- Clear subconscious blocks
- Rewire limiting beliefs
- Receive deep energy healing
- Align with your soul's highest level (timeline)

This whole-body, mind, and soul approach supports quick lasting transformation — for those ready to step into heart-led, frequency-aligned living.

Book a session or learn more:

infinitemindsetcoaching.org

219

220

www.ingramcontent.com/pod-product-compliance
Lightning Source LLC
Chambersburg PA
CBHW070813120626
46556CB00002B/488